"As a book club founder, I have _____, _____ ____ ___
none as compelling and 'in your face' as Susan's book on the different
personality languages. Her book titled <u>Learn How to Make Things
Right by Getting E.V.E.N</u> is an outstanding resource for learning the
basic temperaments of people, understanding the differences and
developing new skills on how to enhance relationships with the added
bonus on how to have a win /win conflict resolution strategy. Her
development of the E.V.E.N method for personality identification and
her I.A.M technique for communication is brilliant and effective. The
learning here can be applied to any aspect of personal, professional
or even casual relationships. A "must have" for anyone in any type of
relationship. A real problem solver hands down."

— Shunda Leigh
Founder/President of Circle of Friends II Book Club
1995-2006

"Susan's program is the Rosetta Stone of personality languages. She
delivers a clear and easy understanding of the complex nature of
interpersonal relationships. It has given me a whole new way to con-
nect with my patients."

— James Gray, M.D.
Cardiology and Integrative Medicine
La Jolla, CA

"While Susan's program is awesome and very effective for communication and the insight to human behavior, plus it's the Holy Grail for
understanding *why people act the way they do*; it is her own unique
personality that is the real winner here. She is a person who walks the
walk and practices what she is preaching. She is being truthful when
she says she is here to serve you. I never met Susan before but she was
willing to help me out as a single mom just because she saw a need I
had and she filled it. She has a way about her that just draws you in
and makes you feel very comfortable very quickly. After taking her
program and learning more about personalities I am a better mother,
daughter, teacher and co-worker for it."

— Jennifer Hazzard
Behavior Therapist

"As a wife, mother of two and a substances abuse counselor I have been able to apply Susan's program to my marriage, family and work environment. As a natural born "know it all" I believed there was nothing anybody could tell me. Boy was I wrong! Learning to speak other's personality language has made me a better communicator which has produced great results at home and at work. The program is simple to learn and easier to apply. Susan will change your life."

— *Carmen Suarez*
Substance Abuse Counselor

"I had a "by-chance" run in with Susan in a restaurant. We began speaking and her words have forever changed my life. Immediately I was able to implement some of the tools and insights that she shared with me and saw change in those around me that night! For me, the most powerful part of this program was not gaining and understanding of other people, but the amount of insight I gained about my own needs and what makes me tick. Since the moment I met Susan, she and the things she has taught me have been in my head like any strong, solid- *works for you every time,* piece of advice.. Whenever I have an issue, I turn to Susan or think to myself, "What would Susan say." Working in the entertainment industry, I run into a lot of conflict with a lot of various personality types. Through the skills I've learned, I'm now able to seamlessly resolve conflict and moreover prevent it from happening when I see the signs. My industry cohorts have noticed such a change in my behaviors that they too have asked for the secret sauce. I've told them all about Susan and her program teachings on I A.M. E.V.E.N. Now knowing Susan personally, I've even gone steps further and referred friends and colleagues to speak with her on a 1:1 basis. They've all come back to me and said how their lives had for ever been changed with the knowledge they received. I hate to sound cheesy, but this stuff works!"

— *Quentin Latham*
Celebrity Blogger and Entertainment Host

Learn How To Make Things Right By Getting E.V.E.N.

Susan Heinemann

Learn How To Make Things Right By Getting E.V.E.N.

Susan Heinemann

Anastacia Media Group

Learn How To Make Things Right By Getting E.V.E.N.

ISBN: 978-0-9829576-6-0

Dedication

I dedicate this book to my family. To my loving, kind and patient husband Bruce, my favorite Remote Control who has taught me to listen more and talk less and to find the good in people – and if I can't, then love them anyway. To my son Taylor, whose sweet, gentle, serving heart has inspired me to rethink my motives and come from a place of love where he says you can't go wrong. To my daughter Katie, who is a mini me, with the exception that she has more talent in her little finger than I do in my entire body; I wish for her to someday soon use her God given talents to influence and inspire others like only she can. To my "second" son Vince for your hard work and dedication to my book, but more importantly the unconditional love you have shown me over the years is very much appreciated. I am proud to call you my loyal friend. To my Heavenly Father, for loving me enough to show me through my trials just who was in control and for teaching me to bubble wrap my Hammer and to do it for His glory. I thank God every day for allowing me the opportunity to increase my faith and take my natural born strengths and use them for good. I thank both God and my family who have been there for me through my transition and continue to love and support me through it all. I am humbled and I love being able to help others check their foundations for cracks and help them to remodel their relationships and live in peace with one another.

Contents

Foreword

Susan Heinemann Four Wires Of You

Being a citizen of humanity comes with a responsibility. Like most people, I possess my own key identifiers: wife, step mother, daughter, sister, boss, best friend, and neighbor. I worked hard my first forty years of life writing my own owner's manual for each role I played in society. Let's face it. Humans aren't born with life instructions. But it wasn't until I got to know Susan Heinemann and her Four Wires of You program, I thought "Wow, this is the owner's manual to life that I have been seeking." As you will learn in this book about your own personalities, I came to understand that I am a primary Remote Control, secondary Tape Measure. As a Remote Control, I look for the shortcuts to make my life easier. I delegate tedious tasks, I look for the fastest route on the map, and in my weakness, I procrastinate doing things that might make my life easier, or even avoid people that overwhelm me.

Thank heavens for Susan and her program. She provided me with the tools to decode my treasured, but often strained, relationships. By learning the simple E.V.E.N. Temperament Theory, I feel like I have a secret weapon, a shortcut, to understanding the cranky woman in front of me at the Deli who insisted that her sandwich be remade because the cheese wasn't completely melted; or the fussy man at the dry cleaners who insisted there wasn't enough starch used on his oxford blue Brooks Brothers shirt. Like a puzzle game, I simply use the tools to identify the personality I am being challenged by, thus allowing me to have a little more compassion for myself and my fellow human beings.

Susan Heinneman's work has also been invaluable for me as a professional. Working with individuals facing loss, I find that understanding the varied personalities helps me comfort and guide them through that experience in a very personal way. We all face life challenges differently, each in our own humbly, stumbling ways. In the end, most of us simply wish to be understood and accepted, seen for who we are and recognized for our own unique place in life. As I have learned to be less frustrated by people who "were not like me" or "just didn't get it" I find that I am a far more effective leader in my work. Through my new found awareness I can example and expose others to a different reality. That new awareness becomes a portal that often allows other's a safe passage to their own renewed sense of living and loving.

I highly recommend this work. It has enriched my personal relationships, healed my broken relationships, allowed me to let go of those who "try to make me over in their own image" so I can be fully myself. We all have a place in the world we were born into. The Four Wires of You is a key that will open the door of your inner "home," where you can relax in your favorite overstuffed chair and invite your dearest friends, with all their different personalities and quirks, to share time with you. To put it simply, it just makes life better.

Stacey Canfield

MESSAGE FROM THE AUTHOR

My program, *The Four Wires of You*, came about as a result of my quest to learn two things – one was *why people act the way they do* and the other was how my life became the mess that it was after a series of life-changing events in 2007. These two seemingly unrelated questions became inexorably entwined by those life-changing events.

It started with an explosion in my difficult relationship with my teenage daughter that precipitated the end of my twenty-five year marriage after my husband took her side in our ongoing battle and walked out on me with her. This, obviously, led to that first question of why people act the way they do. But that, it turned out, was just the beginning.

Shortly after these head-spinning events, my son – who was attending college on the opposite coast (I was in California at the time) – suffered through a serious health scare. We didn't know at the time if he would survive or have long-lasting life limitations. While my son was still recovering, life handed us another crisis – my soon-to-be ex-husband lost his job.

My entire married life (my husband and I met at college) I had been a stay-at-home wife and mother. I had taken care of every detail of our busy and sometime nomadic life. I was an amazing mover whenever we, as family, decided to pursue greater success for my husband's career. I facilitated the numerous artistic pursuits and educational challenges my children took on. I made a comfortable home, cooked meals, and did volunteer work. But the duty of earning income for the family was my husband's. Our economic security was now in serious jeopardy; ironically, just when we were splitting into two households as I had already filed for divorce (the reason this happened so speedily will become apparent as you read this book and get to know my primary personality type – the Hammer). As far as God and the universe were concerned, I apparently still wasn't getting the message.

The cherry on top of the mud sundae was the loss of our home and all of our belongings – including heirlooms and photos, EVERYTHING gone up in smoke – in the October 2007 San Diego wildfires.

All this occurred in roughly a three month period. Three months and my life were seemingly irrevocably broken. For someone who thrives on controlling everything in my life, I was literally brought to my knees. I railed at the injustices and wondered why all of this was happening to me, and us. Then I remembered that God does not give us more than we can handle if we step up to it and I began my search for answers. The answers to why people behave the way they do and how my life had become such a mess. I began my journey toward insight that changed my life, as well as the life of others with whom I have shared it with so far. It is my hope that my journey, which I share in this book, and the insights it gave me will help you, the reader, out of messes that are a lot less traumatic than mine. But if they are equally or more traumatic, know there is a way out.

So, here's a sneak peak – my marriage is still going strong (31 years now), my relationship with my daughter is vastly improved, my son is healthy and successful, and I have started a new chapter of my life feeling empowered, happy, and having a lot of fun! I call it finding the treasures in the trials. And if I (a Hammer) can do it, anyone can.

The Four Wires of You program is not intended to provide an in-depth psychological examination of human behavior; instead, it offers guidelines for understanding and adjusting to the differences in people based on observations of their behavior. My program will give you the tools to enable you to see yourself and your world through someone else's eyes and ears. That insight will go a long way for building compatibility and healthy, happy and more peaceful relationships.

Susan Heinemann
Relationship Remodeler

Introduction to
The Four Wires of You

Do you understand the words that are coming out of my mouth? How many times a day, a week, a month, do you feel like this when trying to communicate with someone? Do you feel like you are speaking the same words but using different dictionaries for translation of these words? If you are human and have a pulse and can fog up a mirror when breathing, then this happens to you often throughout the day.

I devised The Four Wires of You personality identification and communication program as a result of my personal wake-up call, or as I affectionately call it, my "meetin' with Jesus" of 2007. It started from the insight that was given to me as I fell to my knees in front of the remains of our fire-destroyed home from the San Diego wildfires of 2007. I had already begun to see that the common denominator in every mess was me, and even though I may not have had control over some of the circumstances such as the fire, my son's health or my husbands' job loss, the rest of it definitely had my fingerprints all over it. It didn't click just how responsible I was until God sent me a message as I balanced on the knees I had fallen onto while looking, specifically, at the foundation of my family's home. As I asked why it had happened and what I could do, He said into my head "fix your foundation." He did not say fix THE foundation but YOUR foundation. It took me a year to figure out what He meant.

Over the next year I set about learning everything I could find on communication and psychology. It was this study into the ancient wisdom about natural-born personality types (I became a certified personality educator) that finally made it clear to me what God was saying about the why of my mess and how I could go about repairing it. I set out to learn about the different filters we use when we are processing people's words and actions by studying everything I could get my hands on. After that I traveled the country interviewing random people and observing others in conflict. What I learned was that understanding the language of each personality and applying what I call the "platinum rule" (get what you want by giving others what they need) helps us repair our relationships, get what we want, and avoid our worries. It also helps us understand and take advantage of our strengths and stop wallowing in our weaknesses (strengths taken too far) and live better lives.

Since I began using the knowledge and methods set out in this book over five years ago, my husband and I have reconciled and celebrated our 31st wedding anniversary, my husband has an even better job than before, my daughter and I have repaired our relationship, and my son is in good health, has graduated college, and embarked on the career he planned. I owe it all to learning about myself and about others and their personality-driven needs and how they go about fulfilling them. It also helped to have God speak directly to me even though it took a lot for Him to get my attention. When you understand my personality type (Hammer) you will understand completely why it took so long for me to get it.

Origin of Personality Typing

Over 2000 years before Christ came to this Earth, there was a Greek philosopher and physician named Hippocrates. He is known today as the father of medicine. He began to notice that not all people were alike. He noticed that they had different eye and hair color, height, and build, as well as different personalities that set them apart from one another. He noticed that while some people were very happy and upbeat, others were negative and moody, and others were of high energy and angered easily, while yet another group of people were just very calm and relaxed and nothing seemed to stir them up. He believed that he could group these different personalities based on the imbalance of certain bodily fluids, which was the current thinking on the causes of disease. Hippocrates did this around 400 B.C. It was a Greek physician named Galen that expanded upon Hippocrates' theory in 190 A.D. He labeled the four basic personalities with Greek terms based on the assumed fluid imbalance and assigned to them colors and a definition of the effect of the imbalance – this theory was named the Four Temperaments Theory:

Yellow Bile	Yellow	Sanguine
Blood	Red	Choleric
Black Bile	Blue	Melancholy
Phlegm	Green	Phlegmatic

Support from Modern Medicine?

Though we know now that our personalities are not caused by the varying levels of four body fluids, we have confirmed that our personalities are caused by the physical combination of our genes. Recent science in the study of genomics has discovered that our personalities are indeed linked to a different physical source: our genes. For example like our eye and hair color, we inherit our personalities. No man millions of years ago could have thought up the idea that thirty thousand genes make up a human being, and yet our Greek friends were not completely wrong when they suspected that human personalities are linked to our physical makeup.

The Modern Personality Tools

The Four Wires of You program is based on the ancient theory, but it is updated in a myriad of ways. In this program our personalities are still broken into four basic types, but instead of the ancient Greek terms, I have used tools to represent the four basic personalities. I have done this to keep with the theme of looking at your foundation and your relationships and, if need be, using the tools to repair any cracks. In other words, you use these "tools" as part of a Do-It-Yourself relationship and communication improvement project.

The personality "tools" are also expanded from the ancient theory to provide more knowledge and insight than just the overarching mood of the type. The Four Wires – or Tools – go beneath the mood and actions to explain what motivates the mood and behavior. The deep-seated needs of the Tool are illuminated giving insight into your own feelings and choices, as well as of those people around you.

The elements of The Four Wires of You program that this book covers are:

1. The E.V.E.N. personality identification Method + Bonus Clues *The Personality Language

2. How Strengths Can Lead to Struggles

3. The I. A.M. communication technique for effective communication – speaking the language the listener can hear

4. The 4 Wires indicated by tool and color

BASIC CHART

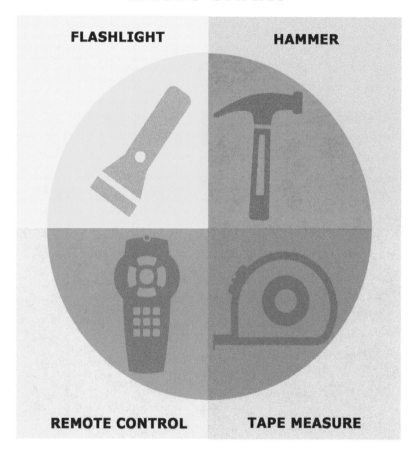

After learning the basics of E.V.E.N., the bonus clues, and I. A.M., we will delve into the details of applying these techniques to each personality type. The application of these techniques are organized by personality tool/type so that you can both gain a deep understanding of them and so that you can reference them again and again to help you identify the people in your life: spouse, children, co-workers and the people you come across in everyday life – like people in the checkout line at the supermarket, customer service for your credit card, and the sales people everywhere trying to sell you something.

One thing that will be important to keep in mind as you read this book is that we are not just a single personality type. We and everyone else also has a secondary personality. How much of "you" is that secondary personality varies by individual. You can play around with this book to try to figure out your own primary and secondary personality and those of others, or you can go to (and send others) http://thefourwiresofyou.com/ and take the FREE test and either get a head start or confirm your analysis.

Chapter 1
Identifying the Personality Types Using The E.V.E.N. Method

Each of the four tools/personality types is exemplified by behavioral, physical, and psychological characteristics. Here is a simple explanation for identifying the different tools with a quick look at the more obvious characteristics. We all naturally identify people by their struggles not their strengths, thus these particular tool icons are used. To keep with the understanding of being born with a natural "hard wiring" each tool is also assigned a wire color. Your personality has a lot to do with how you identify the personality types either by the tool icon or the wire color. Neither is right or wrong, just different. Feel free to use either identification method. For the purpose of my personality I use the tool icons for this book. I will speak about the tool icons in this order below: (**See Basic Chart on Page 21**)

Flashlight/Yellow Wire – This personality type needs the spot light on them. Can be attention-seeking.

Hammer/Red Wire – This personality type needs to be right and will "hammer you" until they make their point.

Tape Measure/Blue Wire – This personality type has a list of unwritten rules that they use to measure themselves as well as others to a higher standard.

Remote Control/Green Wire – This personality type needs to recharge their batteries and will do so with an activity that has an on and off switch. Most likely they will recharge in front of a television. They will take action to control their peace.

The characteristics of each different personality type are organized into an easy-to-remember acronym – E.V.E.N. Here is what E.V.E.N. stands for:

E.V.E.N.
Method

E. Emotional Needs are core necessities that our personalities depend on for emotional well-being.

V. Visual, Vocal, Verbal clues to identify the personalities.

E. Environmental Needs of the different personalities for their success.

N. Natural Desires is the place where your personality operates.

E.V.E.N. As Your Dictionary

Have you ever noticed at times that you feel like you are speaking the same words as your: (a) spouse, (b) child, (c) co-worker, (d) friend, (e) all of the above, but the effect tells you that you must be using different dictionaries? The components of E.V.E.N. that will be introduced to you in more depth shortly are not only clues to help you identify your own and other people's personality types; they are the dictionary for the "languages" that we are all speaking and not understanding.

The languages that our personalities speak are made up of our hardwired emotional and environmental needs, our different natural desires, our different methods of control, and our personal strengths and struggles. For example, your personality may have the natural desire for peace (<u>Remote Control</u>) while your spouse needs perfection (<u>Tape Measure</u>), and maybe your son needs fun (<u>Flashlight</u>) and your mother-in-law needs control (<u>Hammer</u>). None of these desires are wrong or better than the other, just different, and because they motivate our actions and communications they can cause conflict.

No One Needs to Change, but Maybe We Can All Make Small Adjustments

Can you think of people in your life that you would like to change or have even tried to change? People who are too pushy, too critical, too complaining, or too self-centered? Others who frustrate you with procrastination or the high drama of messy lives? Does communicating with these people seem to have you wanting to just walk away because it seems like these people will never change? But are they really the ones who need to change?

As I studied what makes people tick during my personal journey, I came to the realization that once we give up trying to change people and accept that they are just hardwired to be the way that they are, we can be open to understanding and improving our relationships with them. The same applies to accepting ourselves.

So instead of learning E.V.E.N. and the personality type/ tools with the goal of changing someone else – or even yourself – consider it knowledge to help you better **get what you want by giving others what they need** rather than behaving in our default manner of giving others what we want instead of what they need. This is what I call the Platinum Rule. That is not about change, but having the tools to better communicate with each other. How we do this we'll cover more in-depth with the I. A.M. communication technique.

"E" = Emotional Needs

We most always behave in ways that will help us achieve our hardwired emotional needs as these are the core necessities that our personalities need for emotional well-being. These are not wants or desires, or even things we choose, but rather are needs that are hardwired into our personality. When these emotional needs are not met in the way we need them to be met we are more likely to do whatever it takes to ease the pain that occurs when these needs go unfulfilled.

We all are so used to the Golden Rule of giving and doing unto others based on our wants, with no real regard for others' needs. When dealing with communication it is imperative that we practice the Platinum Rule of giving others what they need. This cannot be more important than when we are in relationships with people who are different personalities than our own. Identifying and knowing one's emotional needs is the first step to speaking others' personality language. Once you can identify the personality of the people with whom you live or work and adjust your expectations of them you are really ready for some important transformations.

I can share with you the very day that I had some answers to *why I act the way I do*. I was sitting in my training class for my certification on the personalities. They were explaining the basics on the Hammer and the moment I heard the word loyalty I started to cry because it confirmed that I wasn't just some cold-hearted person. I used to feel that people were not my friend for one reason or another and my feelings got hurt; I would sever the relationship and never feel bad about it. I remember thinking that not being friends with me was their loss. I started to think I was just cold-hearted. After hearing about my emotional needs, I understood that they are my core necessities that I need for emotional wellness, and I operate out of them. Things started to come together with what I had heard that day as I stood on the cracked foundation where my home used to stand before the wild fires took it: "fix your foundation." My core emotional needs were not being met and I was acting out in unhealthy ways to get my "emotional needs tank" filled up. I realized they are needs, not wants. By understanding this I was able to exchange destructive behavior for a healthy behavior. I managed to live through my emotional needs not being met; however but not without a cost, as mentioned before in the introduction.

When our emotional needs are not met, an internal panic starts, which propels us into behaviors that may be harmful to us. Right or wrong, we tend to latch onto behaviors that mislead us into thinking we can breathe again, when in reality these behaviors are sucking the life out of us. Too many of these will be referred to as dysfunctional behavior. (**See Emotional Wellness Checklist on Page 28**)

When we address our emotional needs, we can calm the internal panic. This calm or peace is essential to healthy living. It is necessary to know your emotional needs because it is impossible to work on your strengths and struggles and make behavior modifications and understand conflict resolution until we have our emotional needs met. It is also important to know and understand your secondary personality because those emotional needs should be taken into consideration as well.

As we become aware of each personality's emotional needs and how to best fulfill those needs for others, we can monitor our own emotional health by watching our own behaviors. Stealing our emotional needs from others is an indication that all is not well in our lives. Let me give an example of stealing others' emotional needs.

EMOTIONAL WELLNESS CHECKLIST

Flashlight

Excessive / Compulsive Talking
Using sex as a replacement
for affection,
Overextended-too many activities
Eating (especially sweets)
to medicate pain

Hammer

Overstepping boundaries
Usurping authority
Arguing every point, never wrong
Needing credit for
everything they do
Having fits of rage

Tape Measure

Obsessive worry or fear
Overly sensitive
Reclusive behavior
Eating disorders, such as
anorexia and bulimia

Remote Control

Compulsive lying
Checked out
("Lights on, nobody home")
Physical illness or pain
Becomes passive –
Easily bullied or abused

Stealing Others' Emotional Needs

A common personality conflict occurs between a Hammer parent and child. Both are in need of control, but the "bigger" Hammer (the parent) wins. But the win only lasts in the short run.

The Hammer parent will be in control of everything and when the parent Hammer feels threatened by child Hammer they will tighten the reins by having fits of rage and arguing every point, never being wrong. The child Hammer will seem to buckle under the parent's control, but in fact will act passive aggressively to undermine the Hammer parent's orders by acting out: not following directions completely and acting in other ways to disobey indirectly. The child will also work to be in control in other areas of their life to make up for the lack of control at home. They will act out at school and with their friends.

One of the biggest fears of a Hammer parent is having a rebellious child (a child they can't control); seeing it play out when the Hammer parent reacts to the calls from the school or the parents of other children, the Hammer child will eventually step up the game and take advantage of this fear on the home front. This is not a malicious plan by the Hammer child, but the child playing out his own need for control. The Hammer child will act out big and over the top. Then it will backfire.

It backfires because the natural hardwiring of the Hammer is confidence and self-control, and they believe that they are supposed to rise above the standards that are set for everyone else with regards to morality and making wise decisions. Once the child realizes that their behavior has finally brought the Hammer parent to their knees and they now have the control they thought they wanted, they are miserable. They have to now look in the mirror and ask themselves "What have I done? I used to be a leader and now I am a follower and I have little if any of my natural born hardwiring of self-respect left. Where have my wires gotten crossed?" This journey back for the Hammer to regain self-respect and confidence is a long journey, one that will be impossible unless the Hammer parent adjusts their own behavior.

The key to changing the parent-child dynamic depends on the adult Hammer learning to forgive, giving up some of their control, and showing the child Hammer that they are human. The Hammer parent has to show the child that they too hurt and that they are not perfect. It is difficult for any Hammer to show their emotions, but in the end this will enable the two Hammers to have a respect for each other's emotional needs. There will no longer be a need to steal the other's need for control. It is odd, but once the Hammer gives up the control and learns to control themselves instead of others they will gain all the control they want through giving others what they need. In summary, giving up the negative control gives both of the Hammers more of a healthy control.

The above example illustrates what can occur between two Hammers, but emotional stealing occurs between other personalities and they don't have to be of the same type. It happens when a personality has its emotional needs squelched to the degree that it causes them to act out in unhealthy ways to get what they need. It is very important to take responsibility of your own well-being. It is not healthy to put someone else in charge of you getting your own needs met, but it is something we humans tend to do without thinking. Once armed with the knowledge in this book, you can start training yourself and the people in your life not to do that. In my life, for instance, it is not my natural Hammer hardwiring to give others affirmation, but it is the emotional need of my Remote Control husband and son. It is something that I have to consciously do to ensure that the people I love are happy and so am I. You can also use the knowledge provided by my E.V.E.N. Temperament Theory as a tool for healthy, happy relationships with yourself and with others.

Since each personality has distinct emotional needs, it will take a little bit of practice to step outside of who you are and what you want, to then look at the other person and change your approach to them. This is where real growth takes place in relationships. Once you process this you will find that you can use this insight with all of your interactions, not just those closest to you but with complete strangers like the cashier at your local grocery store or perhaps your child's teacher or the new client you are trying to work with.

As we review the emotional needs of each personality, think about your own emotional needs of both your primary and secondary personality type. What do you need? Are you getting those needs met in a healthy way? Ask the same questions about the people you care about or the person you are in conflict with.

Relationship Remodeler says: "Do not give someone else the job of making you happy. People will let you down every time. Take control of having your own emotional needs filled. Get what you want by giving others what they need."

"V"= Visual clues

It is awkward to go up to someone and ask "Will you take this free test so I can figure out what personality type you are?" They will more than likely look at you like you are crazy. Luckily, we can identify them without the benefit of the personality profile test. If you watch and listen to people you will be able to clearly identify their primary and secondary personalities. People will show you how they want to be treated because we all give what we need. Just look and listen, it will take some practice but you will be able to identify them by visual, vocal and vocabulary clues.

Once you have read the visual clues for each type/ tool, you will be able to identify the primary personality and maybe the secondary personality of the people with whom you live or work. I trust that reading over these traits will help you to know your own personality more objectively. Just try and imagine how you would describe someone if you were trying to fix them up on a blind date. Would you say they are quiet, tidy, and closed (Tape Measure) or maybe you would describe their body language as open (Flashlight)? How would you describe your friends if you were going to set them up on a blind date? How would they describe you?

The Second "E" = Environmental Needs

Each of the different personality types has an environmental need, or in other words, the condition of the immediate world around them – the space, the mood, and relations with the people who have an impact on their lives. If the environment is conducive to the particular personality type, he or she will improve their chances for success and satisfaction. Each personality type will have different natural tendencies. Our tendencies are our comfort zones – the area where we feel the most comfortable. As we face daily situations, our feelings will search out areas of comfort and safety. When we know and understand ourselves better we can then put ourselves in the proper environment that will promote our natural tendencies, which in turn will propel us towards success and satisfaction. The opposite is also true: when we are not in an environment that is our comfort zone, we will become frustrated and do what comes natural for our individual personalities under pressure.

"N" = Natural Desires

Our natural desires are the places from which we operate. It is the mood that we try to achieve in everything we do.

For example, my primary personality is a Hammer and my secondary personality is a Flashlight. I will primarily operate out of my natural desire for control when I am in my "Hammer mode." When it gets to be too much (for me, "too much" is when too much detail on a project is required of me), then I resort to my secondary personality where my natural desire is for fun. When I realize I can no longer control the process because too much detail is required, I will go to having fun and walking away. When I feel the pressure of not being in control, I notice this sequence of events takes place. First, I will become agitated and frustrated and go to my method of control, which for the Hammer is anger. I will then be short and quick-tempered because my natural desire is for control. I am obviously not feeling like I am in control when too much detail is involved and I am not completing the task. I then realize that I am becoming out of control which makes it worse, so I will resort to my second natural desire (arising from my secondary personality of Flashlight) which is for fun. I start making jokes and I pull back. I usually quit and figure out another way to get the task done. I have to physically walk away from the problem and go do something fun.

Fun for the Flashlight when under stress can be shopping. You can always tell which months I am under stress – You will see on my debit card account many purchases and many returns. I will purchase under stress and then as the stress subsides I will return what I purchased because the practical side of my Hammer kicks in and realizes that I did not need that purchase. Imagine how bad this situation could be if I did not understand myself and my actions. This is how Flashlights get in trouble, because their stress reducer is shopping or eating sweets. The combination of emotional needs and natural desires not being met can be traced back to your level of frustration for yourself which results in you acting out.

Using E.V.E.N. Method For Identification

You should be able to give the people who are interacting with you what they need by applying my E.V.E.N. Temperament Theory. You can identify their personality type through my method and then make the adjustments to get what you want by giving them what they need. The other point to make is that when you are aware of your own emotional needs and natural desires, you are able to control the situations you put yourself into to avoid not having your needs met. Self-discovery is important to understanding the role you play in the miscommunications in your relationships and possibly your own self-imposed frustration. The combination of E.V.E.N. is the personality language we all speak. To learn E.V.E.N. is to learn the different personality languages we all speak.

For me, I can trace my actions back to the fact that either my emotional needs or natural desires were not being met. Still, I know that I am the only one responsible for my actions and that is extremely empowering – for my Hammer personality type, which fulfills my need for control. Likewise, knowing the emotional needs and natural desires of others helps you avoid miscommunication by giving others what they need. Understanding the place from which we operate is powerful and is crucial for removing the constant question "Why do they act that way?" Identifying the natural desire is one more tool for you to use to achieve more fun, control, perfection, and peace for yourself and for your relationships.

Applying these principals is like refining your personality. I am not asking you to become somebody you are not naturally hardwired to be, but to build on who you are naturally. Keep it real. Trying to become somebody you are not born to be is expensive and mentally exhausting. Think about it in these simple terms: If you are born with naturally straight hair and you want curly hair, you will spend time, energy and money trying to obtain curly hair – maybe with perms, hot rollers, or a curling iron. But all of these options come with a price: they are expensive, time-consuming and damage to your hair. Trying to be someone you are not is exhausting and the damage often comes in stress-related illness.

Chapter 2
Bonus Clues

In addition to the elements of E.V.E.N., The Four Wires of You also provides what I like to call the "bonus clues" to help us understand and identify the personality types of ourselves and others. Knowing these added items of information gives us a deeper wealth of information to know ourselves and help us get along with – and even get what we want from – others.

The Bonus Clues for each personality type are:

1. Struggles & Strengths
2. Methods of Control
3. The Questions Each Type Want Answered

Just to be clear, while the Hammer personality is characterized primarily by a need to control his or her environment, circumstances, and even people around them, all of the personalities desire some level of control to get what they need; they just use different methods to achieve it.

1. Struggles and Strengths

Strengths are one of the "bonus clues" that comprise our personalities and help us not only identify the type, but also provide more information that we can use to decrease our personal anxieties and improve our relationships by allowing us to adjust our expectations and our approaches. So what exactly are the strengths? Strengths are the things that our hardwiring makes us really good at and, if you are not masking (pretending to be another personality type – perhaps because a parent imposed their personality type on you during childhood or because of workplace pressures), you rely on these to get by and get ahead. Understanding these strengths in ourselves and in others is empowering, but taking them too far can actually make life more difficult and create more struggles.

When we delve into each personality type, we can see the strengths and struggles that are unique to each. As you read about these, I encourage you to take off the rose-tinted glasses and really take a look at the own strengths <u>and</u> struggles of your personality. Being honest with yourself will help you get the most value out of this program.

I love this section when I am teaching live. It goes a little like this: Mother and daughter sitting in back row. Mother says, when we are reviewing her personality strengths "Oh yes, that is me!" Daughter then beams and says with pride when we are reviewing her strengths "Oh, I do that. Yes, it's my biggest strength!" Then when it comes to the struggles portion both become quiet, but will nudge each other with their elbows while their arms are crossed tightly around their own waists. It is not often that I hear someone say with enthusiasm "Oh, yes, that is me, I am guilty of acting that way" when we are discussing struggles. The truth is, though, it takes work to live in your strengths. That is why most of us will recognize each other by our struggles, not our strengths.

As you look at your own personality, your goal should not be to use your struggles as your excuse for bad behavior. Your goal should be to maximize your strengths and minimize your struggles. As the saying goes "accent the positive, eliminate the negative." Do yourself a favor and refrain from saying, "I cannot help it. I am hardwired this way, so just accept it." This attitude will never help you and it will keep you from being the best you can be. As you mature, the goal should be for you to move into the strengths of all the personalities, since this provides for a well-balanced individual.

Strengths Carried to Extremes Become Weaknesses

As you look at your own personality and seek to grow, realize that any strength can be carried to an extreme. Carefully consider whether this might be true in your own life. What you may see as strength, others around you may view as a weakness.

How this applies to me as a (secondary) Flashlight is that I naturally speak in a loud voice. This is good if you are going to make your income as a professional speaker (I do), but not so positive in social settings where I can become brassy and obnoxious. By being aware of my natural tendency I have learned to judge whether the volume of my voice is appropriate or whether it will be a turn off for others. Once you learn how to tone down the extremes of your personality and control the various degrees of your positives, you move beyond just a personality label and head toward the goal of living in your strengths.

What Makes Us Different

When I teach this material live, I have often found that people notice that a person of a specific personality seems very different from another person who is of the same personality. The thing is that we humans are each unique and the differences are explained by our unique experiences, whether we are living in our strengths (or struggles), and, as we will learn about shortly, our secondary personality tool and what percentage of our personality it makes up.

If a person grew up in a home in which they were disciplined and taught right from wrong, their offensive behaviors were probably curbed. However, if a person grew up in a home in which they were allowed to do whatever they wanted, their rough edges were never smoothed. As a child they were out of control – and as an adult, they are living in their weakness.

If you know people of a certain personality who are living in their struggles, they may give you a bad impression of everyone who is that same personality. Refrain from judging all personalities the same, keep in mind they are different depending where they are in their strength or where they are in their struggle.

Once you have a good understanding of your personality – including your strengths and struggles – you can use this knowledge as part of your personality plan to help you get from where you are to where you want to be. As you begin to understand your personality and the personalities of others, you can use this knowledge to keep your extremes under control, live in your strengths and give grace to others. (**See Strengths and Struggles Chart on Page 43**)

2. Method of Control

When we talk about control it usually draws a negative connotation. Each of the personality types has the need to have some sense of control in their lives. It is the method that they use to obtain that sense of control that makes them different.

Can you think of what you do to maintain control in your life? For me, it is anger and at times charm. What is odd is that I am now aware when I use anger to control, but the charm is less obvious to me. However, I am sure that people on the receiving end know exactly when I am trying to control them with my charming ways. Since becoming self-aware, I make a conscious effort to keep both of my natural hardwiring methods of control in check. Relax and understand that all of us have an innate need to be in control. This is just another tool you can use to identify the different personalities and begin to understand what makes people tick by identifying their method of control. In a perfect world, all of our emotional needs, environmental needs and natural desires would be fulfilled and we would have no need for control, but this is not very realistic.

Not an Excuse

Addressing the particular situations in which the individual personalities will exhibit their methods of control is not a free pass to act negatively; it is used to explain the situations that have us using our control methods. I view it as giving you an explanation, not an excuse for bad behavior. If we are asking ourselves constantly *Why do I act this way?* or *Why do they act that way?* then it makes sense to understand the particular situations or environments that have us responding a certain way with regards to our method of control. One of the goals as you look at your own personality is to accentuate the strength and minimize the struggles, not just use the struggle as an excuse for bad behavior. So all Flashlights, Hammers, Tape Measures and Remote Controls, you have now been educated on your needs and *why you act the way you do*, so no more excuses when you use your methods of control of charm, anger, mood swings, or procrastination. You have self-awareness and that is powerful knowledge to have in order to avoid conflict. On the other hand, those of you that are having trouble understanding *Why do they act that way?* also now have the *tools to get what you want by giving others what they need.* Nobody is perfect and there will be slip-ups every now and then; but it won't be like it has been in the past because you are armed with knowledge and the tools to make adjustments for improved relationships.

3. Questions the Personalities Want Answered

The different personality types have different tendencies that come naturally to them. Our tendencies are our comfort zones – the areas where we feel most comfortable. As we face daily situations, our feelings search out these areas of comfort and safety. None is more apparent in how each of us views situations. You have heard how two people could witness an accident and both would be certain they saw things in a particular way and neither would be distorting facts, yet they would be facts to them based on their hardwiring. However, different personalities perceive facts in differing ways. This is what we call a difference in perception. The differences in perceptions can be linked to how the different personalities ask questions. Let's say you are at work and all four personality types are being presented the same "facts" concerning the overall project. The Flashlight will say, "Who all is participating in this project?" The Hammers will ask, "What is the expectation of this project?" Tape Measures will ask like clock-work – and you can set your watches to it – "Why are we doing this project this way, I know a better way?" The Remote Controls will ask, "How do we need to do this project?" Again the issue is not so much the actual information or factual data as it is our perception and perspective regarding that information.

STRENGTHS & STRUGGLES

	STRENGTHS	STRUGGLES
Flashlight	Outgoing, Responsive, Warm and Friendly, Compassionate, Enthusiastic, Talkative	Undiciplined, Emotionally Unstable, Unproductive, Egocentric, Exaggerates
Hammer	Strong Willed, Independent Visionary, Practical, Productive, Decisive,Leader	Cold and Unemotional, Self Sufficient, Impetuous, Angry, Domineering, Sarcastic, Cruel
Tape Measure	Gifted, Analytical, Self-Sacrificing, Industrial, Patient, Sympathetic	Moody, Self-Centered, Persecution-Prone, Revengeful, Unsocial, Theoretical, Touchy, Critical, Negative
Remote Control	Quiet,Easygoing, Dependable,Objective, Diplomatic, Calm Efficient, Organized, Practical, Humorous	Unmotivated, Procrastinator, Selfish, Stingy, Self-Protective, indecisive, Fearful, Worrier

METHOD OF CONTROL

Flashlight

Charm

Hammer

Anger

Tape Measure

Mood Swings

Remote Control

Procrastination

QUESTIONS THEY WANT ANSWERED

Flashlight

Who
as in
"Who will be going?"

Hammer

What
as in
"What is the bottom line?"

Tape Measure

Mood Swings
as in
"Why are we doing this?"

Remote Control

Procrastination
as in
"How do you want this done?"

Chapter 3
Communication:
The I. A.M. Technique

As we have seen in our day-to-day living, our personality impacts our lives. As my motto goes: *Your YOU affects your DO.* Our *"you"* is our personality and our *"do"* is the set of choices we make every day. In other words, our personality impacts every aspect of our lives because every choice we make can be traced back to our natural born hardwiring, including our communication with people. Every day, we communicate with others. It may be with the people at work, the grocery store clerk, the server at the restaurant, our family members. As we communicate – through both written and spoken word – we will inevitably have miscommunications occur.

Understanding that we are all, in effect, speaking different personality languages is a start, but it is not the entire solution to having effective communication. The truth is we are speaking the same words but using different dictionaries. My I. A.M. Technique is the key to translating the different personality languages that we all speak. It is the blueprint – the how-to – for obtaining effective communication by *speaking the language the listener can hear.*

Language creates barriers between people of not only different cultures, but also between different personalities, in the same way that each personality is somewhat of a culture unto itself. When we learn how to accurately interpret as well as speak the "language" of another person, we can bridge the different barriers that divide us from each other, learn how to communicate more effectively, and build better relationships.

We can learn to communicate in the personality languages of others. If I speak Japanese and you speak Chinese, I can learn Chinese and you can learn Japanese so that we can communicate in something other than improvised, poor sign language or gestures. In the same way I speak "Hammerese" and you speak "Remote Controlese," we can learn each other's language to better communicate. Of course, just understanding how our personalities influence our communication will not immediately eliminate every problem that we will have with others. However, by understanding our personalities and the personalities of others and the language they speak, we can use that knowledge to find the root of the conflict and misunderstandings between ourselves and others and determine how to fix those problems.

Three Foundation Flaws

We all behave and communicate with others from the perspective – the needs and make-up – of our individual personality types. Without understanding this about ourselves we are blind to the impact that we have on the quality of our lives and relationships. This is because we all:

1. Give what *we* need, not what *others* need.

2. Judge ourselves on our intentions, but others judge us on our actions and these two things rarely ever line up. The old intentions vs. actions game.

3. Do not speak others' personality language, which leads to ineffective communication and understanding.

This is very human behavior, but when it is done automatically and without the understanding that you will glean in this book, then it causes problems unless you are dealing with someone of the same personality type. The chance that you are surrounded by only your own personality type is virtually nil, and it would make life a lot less full and interesting anyway. Let's take a more in-depth look at what these basic human behaviors entail.

We all give what we need, not what others need

It is very common because we do what comes naturally to us. For example, a Remote Control needs peace, so therefore they give peace. However, if they are married to a Hammer who does not need peace but control, conflict will ensue. The Hammer can view the Remote Control's need for peace as lazy. The Remote Control can view the Hammer as controlling and draining.

As an illustration my friend is a Remote Control and she has a natural desire for peace. I am a Hammer with my natural desire for control. Before understanding each other's personality language we would have struggles when we would go on our girls' getaway weekends. I would be the one making the plans with my need for control of the situation being met. She would be alright with me making the plans because she did not want the extra work of making the plans, her peace need was being met. This was all fine until the actual time came for the trip. I had planned the trip with activities and fun and I believed I was doing the right thing because after all, I would like that if someone did this for me. She needed the trip to relax. I was giving her what I needed, activity and fun. When we were at the hotel and she was taking her time every morning getting ready with no excitement or energy for the day I had planned, my emotional needs of credit for good work and appreciation were not being met. So, I would become upset and like a Hammer have a hard time containing my disappointment. Now that we know and understand the personality languages we make the effort to give each other what we need when doing our friendship affirming girls' weekends and our conflicts have been minimized. I have learned to get what I want by giving her what she needs.

Intentions vs. Actions

The above story about my friend and me on our girls' getaway weekend can also demonstrate the intentions vs. actions theory. I had the intention of making sure our getaway was fun and memorable. However, she was judging me on my actions as being controlling, domineering and selfish. I was judging her on her actions as being lazy, unappreciative, and deliberately being a martyr by not helping make the plans and then resenting them. The definition of a good time was very different for both of us because we speak different "languages." How we solved this problem is by speaking each other's personality language and compromising on our definitions of having a good time. I have learned to relax a little more and she has learned to be more adventurous. She still does not remember all of her toiletries, so we always plan on spending the first few hours of our vacation shopping for her things. We then follow it up with a night of dancing. We have learned to compromise and laugh at our differences.

Speaking the Personality Languages

Just as you would translate a foreign language in order to communicate with someone who does not speak your native tongue, the same applies to communicating with someone who does not share your personality language. The key to effective communication is speaking the language the listener can hear. The combination of one's emotional needs, visual, verbal and vocal choices, environmental needs, natural desires and methods of control comprises what I call your *personality language.* These things act as our unique, natural filters to understanding the world around us. It is through our individual personality language that we interact in the world and through which we experience people, things and events in the world. You have to be able to speak the particular personality language that corresponds to that of the person with whom you are engaged in a given communication exchange. Effective communication leads to healthy, happy, productive relationships that are moving forward, not standing still or moving backwards.

We all have things we would like to modify about ourselves, but we become frustrated when we do not know where to begin. I can safely and honestly say the key to making these modifications to ourselves as well as to our approach to others whom which we have conflict with, is within an age old secret that we all have heard since we were mere children. However as adults we have a new, updated, put a twist on it way of looking at this old theory. In order to apply this new rule it is imperative that we understand others hardwiring and their particular personality language that they speak for living in our strengths and growing thru our struggles and building better relationships. Are you ready for the secret to getting along with virtually everyone?

Golden Rule, Revised

The first thing we need to do is revise the "Golden Rule" of *do unto others as you would have them do unto you* that we've been hearing since we were children. This is a good principle when you were little and someone was kicking sand in your face on the playground, however, as adults it is the very thing that is standing in the way of us having peaceful, stress-free relationships; it is essential to instead practice what I call the "Platinum Rule:"

Do unto others as they need done to them

Much of the stress and conflict we experience on a daily basis arises simply because we all give **what we** need to others, not **what they need** – in other words, not speaking each other's personality language. For example, one of you might need fun and the other person needs quiet, two extreme opposite needs. Can you see how giving a person who needs quiet your need for fun is a recipe for disaster? This can be alleviated, like in the example above with my friend and our girls' weekends, by learning each other's personality languages.

Steps of the I. A.M. Technique for Communicating with Personalities Different than Yours

The I. A.M. technique is centered on the personality types and is the key to getting what you want (emotional need, most often) by giving others what they need (also most often an emotional need).

Identify the personality language through the E.V.E.N. personality identification method. Are they a Flashlight, Hammer, Tape Measure, Remote Control?

Adjust our approach to others and speak their personality language. Do they need appreciation, acceptance, peace, sensitivity?

Meet them in the middle for effective communication by understanding where they are coming from. Learn how to get what you want by giving them what they need.

Step 1 – Identify Personality Type/Tool Using E.V.E.N.

The first thing to do in order to intentionally communicate to achieve positive results is to use the E.V.E.N. method (**E** emotional needs; <u>V</u> visual vocal and verbal clues; <u>E</u> environmental needs; <u>N</u> natural desires) to identify your own and the other person's personality, and therefore their language. I approach people immediately looking and listening for their visual, vocal and verbal clues. I understand that those clues are very much related to their emotional needs. Let me give you an example that we can use to understand how to apply I. A.M.

I approach a woman at a sales counter at Macy's to return a dress that I had bought over thirty days ago. The normal return policy is thirty days, but I had been traveling and hadn't tried on the dress until just a day ago and discovered that the seam on the back line was pulling apart. I know that the customer service manager has the authority to make exceptions for good reasons, but first I have to get to the manager. As I wait in the long line for my turn, I immediately start to look for visual clues to identify what personality type/tool the representative is.

What I see is that her clothes are not loud but more subdued and her overall appearance looks "perfect." I notice she has few facial expressions and appears to be non-contact oriented when she doesn't touch the dress or notice my attempt to shake her hand. I see and sense she has a quiet, neat and tidy, closed energy to her. I am pretty sure that she is a Tape Measure.

Next, I closely listen to her, to the words she chooses, the tone or inflection in her speech, the volume of her voice. I'm already getting a sense of her personality type, but I carefully listen to her words. She starts off with each customer factually, telling them about the return policy and process. Her tone is formal and proper, but there is an edge of being rushed in her tone.

When I get to her and explain my situation she still factually explains the policy, but she also sympathizes with my situation and begins to complain about the hard time she has enforcing the policy with some customers, how busy she is as she glances frequently at the line behind me, and how she can get in trouble if she violates policy even when it makes sense like in my situation. She frequently uses the word "perfect." I am now sure she is a Tape Measure that is living in her struggles and this is because one of her emotional or environmental needs are not being met. I know her emotional needs are sensitivity and that her biggest fear may be that others do not understand what she is going through. I also know that she has an environmental need of having enough time to complete a task and not having that is causing her to complain. I know that calling a manager while she has a big line to contend with challenges that need even more because it will take more time. I also know that her natural desire is "perfection" and doing her job perfectly.

I have just used my E.V.E.N. method to identify her personality and the language it speaks. Next, I will apply the platinum rule of giving her what she needs, not what I need, to get what I want – to be able to return the dress.

Step 2 – Adjust Your Approach

The heart of The Four Wires of You Program is living an easier life by understanding yourself and others and using that understanding to have better communications. Since by now you realize that you can't change other people, this is the step where what *you* do makes the difference and achieves results.

What is Your Personality Language?

Each of us has a primary and most of us have a strong secondary personality, each of which is pre-packaged with a communication style. The Flashlight can talk incessantly whether anyone is interested or not. The Hammer is good at quick commands and keeping conversations geared to just the facts. The Tape Measure is better at listening than talking, sharing on only a need-to-know basis. The Remote Control is a listener, almost preferring to stay uninvolved, seemingly fearful of entering a conversation; yet in times of stress, the Remote Control is the one to talk to as just the sound of his or her voice is calming.

When it comes to communication, each personality type has a number of strengths, but also a number of areas in which improvement is needed. In the following sections, we will take a look at some of the most prevalent areas of strength and struggles and then determine how we best can adjust our approach to communication so that we can communicate more effectively with people who are of a different personality than our own.

Communicating to Others

Remember, communicating with others is not simply just talking or sharing ideas or speaking to others. Communication is a two-way street, but before we communicate effectively we need to know our own strengths and struggles so we can capitalize on our strengths and work on overcoming our struggles. As we work to minimize the distracting communication habits that are part of our personality, communication becomes more effective.

One of the best ways to communicate more effectively is to learn to make adjustments to your natural communication style to meet that of the people with whom you are in communication. I have given you the E.V.E.N. method for identifying the personality you are communicating with, and I now have given you the I. A.M. technique for the adjustments needed for speaking the language the listener can hear – which is effective communication. I have given you the tools for adjusting your approach to the different personalities, rather than relying on your own natural tendencies. Remember, you will succeed at getting what you want by giving others what they need.

Whether your communication is professional or personal, you will find it is enhanced by following the basic communication tips from the I. A.M. section and charts based on your personality. The charts tell you how to adjust your approach to meet others' needs based on their personality. You cannot change other people, but you can change your approach to them. Remember, the E.V.E.N. method identifies the personality and I. A.M. technique is the adjustment tips to speak the listener's personality language for effective communication.

All of us, regardless of our specific personality type, have areas in which our communication is easy and we can operate out of our strengths, and all of us have areas in which we can improve. After you begin to identify your own personality and work toward improving yourself by checking your own foundation first, then you can work on identifying the other personality types and adjust what you say and how you approach them. Give it a try and be ready to enter the amazing world of effective communication.

Step 3 – Meeting in the Middle

Meeting in the middle is what naturally occurs when you have taken the steps to identify someone else's personality and the language it speaks. It happens when you make the necessary adjustment to your personality so they can hear what you are saying when you communicate. It is the result of giving others what they need so you can get what you want. Some may view this as a form of manipulation. It is not, because manipulation is when only one of the parties involved gets what they want and need. By using my I. A.M. technique, both parties are satisfied and an actual meeting in the middle has taken place. It is the art of understanding and compromising and not being selfish that has this method working. You can get your emotional need met by giving others what they need. You can't get what you want until you figure out exactly what it is that you want, nor can you give others what they need until you know what it is that they need. That is why *The Four Wires Of You personality identification and communication program* is effective. You learn through my E.V.E.N. method what it is that you want and also what others need, and the I. A.M technique gives you the tips and tools for effective communication. The end result is meeting in the middle – also known as the WIN/WIN effect.

Getting back to our Macy's example:

First, I've identified the sales clerk's personality type as a Tape Measure. I also understand that my own hardwired desire is to do tasks and solve problems. I do not have much sympathy for what I call complaining. My emotional need is for control; not controlling people, but controlling situations.

The perceived complaining coming from the Tape Measure sales clerk woman would have in the past drove me right up a wall and I am certain would have had my "Hammer" out and ready to tell her exactly how to solve her "problem" by cutting her off and telling her to get the manager immediately (I'm not proud of it, but most likely I would not have considered whatever she is complaining about an actual problem since, to me, if she would just get the manager right away less time would be wasted).

Now that I know the I. A.M. technique I quickly apply it to this potential conflict between my Hammer personality and her Tape Measure Personality. I begin by

I: Identifying her personality language of sensitivity, support and space and silence.

A: Adjusting my approach by saying "I am so sorry you are going through this, it must make you feel frustrated. What do you think we can do about this?"

I would then be quiet and let her talk a little longer and actively listen. If she doesn't come up with a solution and continues to complain, then I know by her actions that she is not interested in solving my (or her) problem and only wants me to understand and feel her pain. I can do that no problem – now. You see, before I would have mistaken the complaining as a request for help, *i.e.* problem solving – a need I have, and I would have tried to control the situation by giving her a solution.

M: Meeting her in the middle is listening, sympathizing, and not solving her problem. I also get to keep my control because I am in control of my emotions and am no longer allowing my naturally hardwired method of control – anger – to rule. I get what I want (control) and she gets what she needs (sympathy and understanding).

If this was a situation with a friend or family member and there wasn't something that I needed right away, I would know that over time, me giving her sympathy and understanding of how she is feeling will open her up to having me help her solve her problems because she now has her emotional need of sensitivity and support being met by me. She would trust that

I do understand what she is going through, so she will be open to hearing solutions that my "big picture" Hammer personality would see and my need would be met for appreciation of my knowledge.

But because I do have an immediate need and this is not a strictly social situation, I would again acknowledge the representative's frustration, using her first name, of course, and ask if I could suggest a solution. I would suggest the she bring the dress to her manger and show him the unraveling seam, that I was upset about the quality of the product, and then put me at a different counter while she continued to service her line. Now that I have acknowledged her fear of getting in trouble, and her frustration at not having the time or authority to do a perfect job, she will most likely agree to my idea and appreciate me for it. Then I would start the process all over again with the manager and get my store credit.

Giving the Tape Measure what she needs not only helps me by getting me closer to returning the dress, it also fulfills my Hammer needs. As you will learn in more detail in the Hammer chapter, the Hammer is a big-picture-seeing kind of person and can often see solutions to problems if they are being appreciated for their knowledge. If the Hammers are not appreciated they will do one of two things: a) become more vocal and aggressive until you hear and take action on what they say – in other words, "hammer you," or b) they will completely cut you out of their lives and not look back; they will be officially "done" with you. I got what I wanted (control of the situation by not becoming frustrated or angry) by giving her what she needed (sensitivity and support). Win/Win!!!

In summary, in this example I applied E.V.E.N. method to identify her personality and the language her personality speaks. I then proceeded to use the I. A.M. technique for effective communication to end with a more controlled (my wants), perfect, sympathetic, supported encounter (her needs). The end result was effective communication – I spoke the language she could hear – and getting what I want.

Chapter 4
The Personality Tools

Let's Meet the
Fabulous Four
Personalities

Let's Meet The Flashlight

The Flashlight

1. **You will notice.** Flashlights are loud, colorful, flashy, expressive and extroverted. They want you to notice them, which explains why they dress the way they do, talk with a loud voice, and aren't afraid of a really good hug. You know them when they walk into a room because they are full of life and a good story – or a bad story – but nonetheless, a story.

2. **There will be drama.** Flashlights are great storytellers and great at making up stories, too. Any normal, mundane event can turn into a theatrical display if a Flashlight is involved in telling the recap. They thrive around people and can usually draw a crowd with their antics. These talkers usually give you far more information than you ever wanted or needed to know, and tend to embellish when they have a captive audience. The thing is, Flashlights are charming and they are funny and you will like them. Most people come to recognize that life would be boring without them around.

3. **There will be fun.** A Flashlight's natural desire in life and motivation for doing most everything is the need to have fun. They work so they can play and they play while they're at work. Spontaneity is their schedule. If something more fun comes along, they will do their best to scrap the plan and go, go, go. Flashlights are energized by people. They

may be physically exhausted, but if you throw them in an environment where there's a crowd, they magically come to life and perform. Flashlights are definitely the life of a party and much desired as a party guest.

4. **There will be disaster.** Unfortunately, the fun doesn't always last. Flashlights are often distracted and forgetful; it is not easy for them to mentally record things that are not fun. And listening is hard. So, things get lost, appointments are forgotten, and instructions are not followed. In addition, the Flashlight genuinely wants to help, loves to volunteer, and can't say "no." The problem is that they forget to show up, lose track of time, or they just can't seem to follow through because they lose focus along the way. Long term commitments are a struggle. Ultimately, the Flashlight generally feels like they are in trouble... again.

5. **There will be reconciliation.** The good news is that Flashlights truly want solid relationships. They love people and are good-hearted toward others. They are really good at apologizing. In fact, Flashlights say they are sorry more than any other personality type. They want everyone to be happy; happy is fun. Sad and angry are no fun. However, Flashlights must be cautious that they don't rely on their charm to always bail them out, never learning true responsibility. Just because you *say* you are sorry does not mean you actually are sorry, and other people know it.

6. **There will be a following.** Flashlights are, after all, popular. They love to lead the parade. They are the world's natural cheerleaders, leading their friends, co-workers and teams with enthusiasm and excitement. People are

persuaded by their optimism, energy, and unique ability to make difficult tasks fun. Flashlights, however, must learn how to listen and manage time wisely if they want to actually get things accomplished. As they say, a little less talk and a lot more action.

7. **There will be emotions.** Flashlights are emotional creatures, just like all personalities. The difference is they aren't afraid to show it. To attain and maintain emotional health, Flashlights *need* attention, affection (in the form of touch), approval of every deed, and acceptance "as is." Flashlights basically need to believe and know that people like them and love them just the way they are. They also feel very insecure if people do not praise them for a job well done. So, give your Flashlight a hug, make sure they know they look good, they did well, and you wouldn't trade them for the world and your relationship will thrive. It really is simple with the Flashlight.

E. V. E. N.
Method
Flashlight

E Emotional Need	Attention, Affection, Approval, Acceptance
V Visual Clues	Loud, Open Cluttered
E Environmental Need	Prestige, Friendly Relationships, Opportunities to influence and inspire others.
N Natural Desire	Fun

BONUS CLUES

Method of Control	Charm
Questions they want answered	Who As in "Who will be going?"
Motto	"It's all about me"

"E" Emotional Needs of The Flashlight

Attention * Affection * Approval * Acceptance

Those of us who are Flashlights come hardwired for attention, affection, approval and acceptance. We are the ones who are most likely to behave in such a way that we demand others to give us what we want. For example, my husband has zero Flashlight traits, but I am about 40 percent Flashlight (Flashlight is my secondary wire after Hammer). Whenever I buy a new outfit and I try it on for him and I need his undivided attention so he can give me his approval, but he almost always says in a non-emotional, monotone voice, "you look fine." Wounded, I say, "Fine? Is that all you got?" Now I realize that he is giving me what he needs – peace and quiet – and clothes do not excite him on any level. There is an easy fix for him to give me what I need, a simple compliment with some enthusiasm behind it. Once he does that, he will get his peace and quiet because all I need is a compliment with enthusiasm and then I will go away.

Attention

One of the Flashlight's biggest fears is that they will become normal and blend in. They like attention and want to be noticed. That is why they dress the way they do and talk with loud voices. It is all for the attention. Flashlights do not get attention in ways they will get it in other ways, negative ways. Just ask any teacher and she will tell you, to a Flashlight there is no such thing as bad attention; it is all attention to them.

My friend is a middle school teacher and she told me this story about a Flashlight student named Chloe. Chloe was a very happy, outgoing child and she loved people and she was very energized by them. When things were going well at home, she would do her homework and made good grades and listened well and was generally pleasant to be around. However, things changed when things at home were not going well.

Whenever Chloe's mom was working a lot of overtime and her dad was traveling a lot for work, Chloe would act out and generally cause disruption in class; she would talk all the time, tell stories that did not always have much truth to them, and she became overly aggressive with the boys in class. My friend would call her mom only to have the mom be curt, telling her that it was the teacher's problem to solve and she was busy doing the best she could.

My friend is a very sympathetic person so she spent that year broken-hearted for Chloe. A few years later she saw Chloe in a store and she called her by name. Chloe was surprised that my friend remembered her name. My friend said, "How could I forget her name… I must have said it 100 times a day saying 'Chloe stop doing that.'"

My personal experience with being partly a Flashlight doesn't have the typical reactions that most Flashlights have when it is their primary personality that they will operate out of. I just had to be careful when my children hit their teen years. I was the pied piper of our neighborhood. I love to entertain so all the kids usually would end up at our house for flashlight tag, kick the can, or attending a fondue party. I needed to be aware of my kids' feelings for needing to be the reason that the neighborhood kids came over to our house, not for me and the attention I showed to them. This was especially hard on my daughter. As teen girls go, she wanted the attention of the boys and it was hard because most of the kids in our neighborhood were boys who did not have moms that were Flashlights who loved to have fun. My intentions were to just show everybody how to have fun, but my daughter did what is natural for her personality: she judged me on my actions. My actions said that I was what my son called a "scene stealer" or a "story stomper." This means a Flashlight may be trying to add to the conversation or increase the "fun," and their action may be judged as seeking too much attention. This will irritate a Tape Measure who most likely will have an unwritten rule that the Flashlight should not be so attention-seeking. I am now aware of my storytelling and my desire to create more fun when I am in the presence of Tape Measure/ Hammer personality types.

Relationship Remodeler says:
Flashlights, be aware of being a "scene stealer" or a "story stomper"

If you have a Flashlight in your life, understand that they want you to notice them. Comment on their clothes, laugh at their jokes, and let them tell the long version of their stories. If you make a habit of this, they will be very forgiving when you occasionally have to tell them you don't have time for the long version because they will already know that you really do like them.

Affection and Approval

Flashlights want to be loved. This is the root of their hugging and kissing everyone they meet. If you know a Flashlight, you know they will reach out and hug you first even if you are uncomfortable with the hugs. If affection is not found in healthy realms, Flashlights will find it elsewhere. It is not that they intentionally determine to make poor choices in order to fill this need, but because these emotional needs are hardwired the Flashlight will subconsciously do what they can to get them met. They will sell their soul for a hug. This is true even if you have a young female Flashlight because if their emotional needs for affection are not met they could wind up looking for love in all the wrong places.

A secondary aspect for Flashlights is the need for approval. They do not want to have their approval hinged on anything specific, like work; they just want to be hugged and told they are fabulous and wonderful people for just being themselves. Affirm them often with colorful adjectives.

Acceptance

How many of you have a Flashlight in your life that you are always trying to fix, shape them up, or get them organized? Flashlights may appear to be disorganized. Because they are visual learners they keep a lot of their things at fingers' reach. They do have a method to their madness. The term "hot mess" can be used to describe a Flashlight. They can be all over the place with their lives. They float from one project or idea to the next with little follow through, in their struggles. Flashlights need you to stop making plans for their lives and just accept them for who they are. Here is something to think about: if you stop trying to change them and simply give them the praise and approval they need, they are more likely to want to make changes to please you. The catch is, they need to feel accepted first.

Be careful that you do not underestimate the emotional need for acceptance for the Flashlight personality. You would hate to see them trade their dignity for attention and acceptance.

Relationship Remodeler says: "Dads, it is very important for you to always show affection and acceptance toward your daughters so they will have their 'emotional needs tank' filled and not go looking for love in all the wrong places. Affirm, affirm and then affirm them some more."

"V" Visual Clues for Identifying the Flashlight

*Loud * Open * Cluttered*
(See Visual, Vocal, Verbal Clue Sheet on Page 182)

Flashlights are first on the list not because they are the most important but because they are the most obvious to identify. Their personalities are so obvious it just radiates out of them. I like to refer to Flashlights as NTN, meaning No Test Needed.

I fly a lot and I am always meeting people in the airport and to me the airport is the best place to people watch (second to Disneyland). Hands down the best airport for people watching is New York's JFK or La Guardia. A couple years ago there was a gate agent named D'Juan. D'Juan was a happy person, and he had some flair to his uniform. His flair was in the form of his hair, his nails and his eye glasses. From his looks and the unique spelling of his name it was obvious D'Juan was never going to blend into a crowd. His hair was dark brown with pink streaks, his nails were painted black, and his glasses were zebra striped. I will give you two guesses as to which airline he worked for and the first one doesn't count. It is the airline that operates on humor and the fun factor.

D'Juan was not only happy and dressed with flair, he was also very loud. His voice was just at a level where you might have thought he was hard of hearing like your Uncle Harold. As he took the passengers' tickets he would say "Blessings to you. Have a great flight." When it came time to take my ticket he looked at what I was wearing and pulled me aside and announced to the other passengers boarding the flight, "Take notice, people! This woman looks fierce, I love to see people who respect travel and bring their best A-game. You go girl!" And with that he gave me a hug and a Hollywood kiss. You see I was wearing my zebra pants and a hot pink off-the-shoulder shirt with my zebra glasses. Takes one to know one I say.

Not every Flashlight will be as easy to spot as D'Juan and I but you can be assured Flashlights will be loud and open in a crowd.

Loud

Flashlights have naturally loud voices that can be heard above the crowd. My personality is about forty percent Flashlight. I have been shushed a few times in my life by more quiet friends, especially if I am telling a story and I think the people in the next table can't hear me. We flashlights love an audience so if we think you are straining to hear us we will talk louder. Just the other day I was at a restaurant by myself having a salad and this little girl Flashlight turned around and smiled at me and asked if I wanted a bite of her chicken. I smiled and politely said no and tried not to look her in the eye because I knew if I did she would not leave me alone until I engaged her in conversation. I was not being mean; I just knew her mother would not appreciate her talking and not finishing her lunch. It did not matter what I did or did not do, this little girl sensed I was a Flashlight too and she wanted me to listen to her story. She started talking to me and I just nodded my head, which was so hard because she was as cute as a bug and I wanted to engage her and get her talking because I know from experience that Flashlight kids have the funniest stories. She could see I was only half listening so she got louder and louder until it was impossible to ignore her. Her mother was so embarrassed (mom was a Tape Measure) that she said "I am sorry, I don't know what I can do with her, she insists on talking with everyone." I smiled and gave her my card and said "It is alright, there is nothing wrong with her and nothing needs to be done. It is her natural hardwiring and I would love to talk more with you about learning to speak her personality language. I for one would love to hear her stories but I can see it might upset you." The little girl spoke up and said "We are going to Stan and Fran's disco for bcation". I nearly fell over laughing because I understood exactly what she was saying, San Francisco for vacation. To think her mom thinks something is wrong with a loud and open adorable Flashlight!

To make it easy to identify Flashlights, just listen to them. Flashlights will have a high pitch and lots of vocal inflection in their voice and a variety of vocal quality in the tone of their voice, as well as dramatic high volume and fast speed. They can digress from the conversation and drift into other side conversations, all the while using terms most often found on UrbanDictionary. com. They have a tendency to "get wound up" when they are talking, which will result in all of the above with factored in great facial and body movements of talking with their hands in big open movements and touching you when they talk. Flashlights are hard to miss when they are telling one of their great stories – it is akin to watching a good sitcom.

Loud clothing is another visible sign of a Flashlight. They will not blend; clothes, hair, nails, whatever it takes. While women have a little more freedom to dress in loud colors and loud prints, men will find a way not to blend in as well. Look closely and you will find they have on a whimsical, loud tie, or socks with polka dots or maybe suspenders.

My son had a fourth grade teacher named Mr. Staples he was a NTN (no test needed) Flashlight. He had a loud voice, his ties were always crazy, and for Halloween he would dress up in a full-on Girl Scout uniform with knee socks and loafers, wig – he left nothing out of the ensemble. As you can imagine, he was – and still is – almost every kid's favorite teacher.

Open

The other visual marker for the Flashlight is their openness, their mouth for starters. They are uncomfortable with dead air and often feel compelled to fill the silence. The open mouth trait has given the Flashlight the moniker "the Talker."

I personally hate to sit on the phone while you are trying to make a doctor appointment and they are pulling up your information. The dead air and silence makes me feel uncomfortable. I also hate it when you have to call your cable company. It is torture for me not to ask the operators how their day is going, where they are located, and anything else that slows down the call because I really am interested in knowing about them and them knowing about me. My secondary Flashlight personality wants to stand out from the other callers.

Not only do the Flashlights have an open mouth, but they also have an open life. They have no secrets and if you do have one, it is best not to tell a Flashlight unless their secondary personality is strong in the keeping things secret and private. I, for instance, have the Hammer primary personality and since I need loyalty I naturally give it. This sharing of secrets is not a malicious act on the part of the Flashlight, it is simply that they have no secrets themselves so it does not register with them to keep your secret a secret. Flashlights just have little, if any, filter between their brain and their mouth. It's up to the other personalities to be aware and careful about that.

If you are talking with someone and they are sharing very personal details of their life – details you probably have no business knowing – you might be talking with a Flashlight. The term TMI (too much information) is coined after the beloved Flashlight.

The Flashlight has an open mouth and an open life, and they also have an open body language. They are very touchy-feely with hugs and kisses. They usually run towards you with open arms as if they haven't seen you in years when in fact they most likely just saw you last week. They can hold onto you while they are telling a story just in case you try and make a run for it before they are finished with their story. I am guilty of this at times.

Cluttered

Another visual clue is the cluttered personal space of the Flashlight. It can be their home, car, or office space. Have you ever seen the car of a person who looks as if they are living out of their car because it is littered with every type of fast food wrapper from the last month? This is most likely the car of a Flashlight.

I had the opportunity of helping a friend one night during the Christmas holiday to decorate for the company she worked for. I was amazed at how each person's office cubicle was a reflection of their personality. One particular cubicle stuck out, it was littered with personal paraphernalia. There were pictures of her family, vacation photos, and even a troll doll collection. It was hard to actually see these things because of the clutter on her desk. I knew right away this was a Flashlight. Flashlights are very visual and if we put things away in a drawer we might forget about them. If you are a Flashlight and want to decrease some of your clutter and still stay productive you can do what I have done – I have color coded my files and they are hanging on my wall in a wall file holder.

Let's review: The keys to identifying the Flashlight are loud voice and loud clothing; an open mouth and open life and body language; and personal space that is littered with personal paraphernalia. If you found someone with these traits, you have found yourself a Flashlight.

Second "E" Environmental Needs Of The Flashlight

*Prestige * Friendly Relationships * Opportunities to Influence Others * Opportunities to Inspire Others * Chance to Verbalize*

Prestige

Flashlights like to be important; they do not like small jobs or small tasks. They like to start at the top. They care more about a title and status than they do raw power.

Friendly Relationships

They are friendly and seem to talk or wave to everyone they see. They know no strangers. Flashlights are compassionate. They tend to act before they think. Sometimes they will give you the shirt off their back, only to discover it is cold outside.

Opportunities to Influence and Inspire Others

They can sell ice to an Eskimo. They make everything sound great. They can influence you with their charm. Flashlights make great front line people for any organization. Flashlights are inspiring; that is, they make things happen. They are cause agents.

Chance to Verbalize Ideas

Flashlights can sometimes be over-bearing because they are so talkative. They seem to know a little bit about everything – or at least they make you think they do, giving you their opinion or point of view on any topic. They are visionaries and do have great ideas; let them verbalize them, but keep in mind they have a hard time taking their ideas to completion.

Relationship Remodeler says: "The key issue for Flashlights is control; it all depends on whether you are in control or out of control. Being in control has great value to you and to others, while being out of control serves no one."

"N" Natural Desire Flashlight

The natural desire for the Flashlight is fun. Just think about it: fun. Now is that such a bad thing to have as your natural desire? Just be careful not to carry it to the extreme. Balance is the key here. The first thought for the Flashlight is fun – and who is going to be involved. Fun is the natural and basic desire for the Flashlight.

Bonus Clues

Method of Control – Charm

Flashlights will control their situations with charm. They will make everyone their new best friend. They love to be liked so they will compliment you and be little Miss Sunshine to get control of a situation.

To review, the Flashlight's emotional needs are attention, affection, approval and acceptance, and their natural desire is fun. If our emotional needs are being challenged we will attempt to exert control. Tips for meeting these needs for the Flashlight are to be authentic with your praise and compliments, listen even when they ramble, don't withhold an appropriate hug, pat on the back or high five. Let them have fun and plan fun for others when it is appropriate. Some situations that can have the Flashlight searching for control include when they think life is no fun and no one seems to love them, or if they feel like people are criticizing them and not responding to their humor or don't think they're cute. If they are operating out of their fear of being unpopular or bored, having to live by the clock, or having to keep a record of money spent, they will super charge the efforts to control through charm. This is natural for them. Try to see them for less of what they do and more for who they are; try a personal connection. Also, don't let them minimize issues; lovingly let them know you need their sensitivity to the situation at hand. In children, the controlling by charm is very obvious but can be harder to detect in adults.

Questions The Flashlight Wants Answered

The Flashlight thinks in terms of "*Who?*" *Who is going? Who will be there? Who will I see? Who will I know?* They are motivated by the emotional need of attention (Who will recognize me?), the social interaction (who can make this fun?) and natural desire for fun. The Flashlight stands out in a crowd. It is impossible to give them too much attention. Remember the thought pattern of "who," the emotional need for attention, and the natural desire of fun or social interaction and you will be speaking their language.

Struggles

The Flashlight Struggles
(See Strengths and Struggles Chart on Page 43)

Emotions: Egotistical

Flashlights can be energetic or enthusiastic, but sometimes these great traits can evolve into weaker traits like egotism or pride.

One of my clients has a tendency to "bite off more than she can chew." She is full of energy and enthusiasm when taking on new projects. However, it is her ego and pride that has her not completing her task or projects.

She recently purchased a foreclosed home and was very excited at taking her first step toward becoming an investor. Her father was a builder so she grew up in the trades and was comfortable with accessing needed home repairs. In her typical mode of operation she has a tendency to underestimate the time it will take her to complete a project. She had a home inspector conduct an inspection with a written report. She neglected to read the report because she knew what the home needed. Her own inspection of her newly purchased home showed the house needed a new roof, some minor hardwood floor repair and paint. She was very confident that she could wrangle up some trades people that would work for next to nothing because after all, times are tough and people should be hungry for work.

She was eager to start her home improvements. Or so she thought -- Her energy, enthusiasm and confidence backfired because she was really operating out of ego and pride.

The inspector's report that she did not read, stated the house had termites. The roof also needed repairs to the garage, and there was structural damage to the foundation which is why her hardwood floor had issues. She also needed to replace the windows because of termites. Remember those trades people that would be hungry enough to work for next to nothing? Well, let's just say they took half of her deposit and fled town.

What should have been a two week repair period and cost less than ten thousand dollars, took her six months and about forty thousand dollars. This entire situation could have been avoided if she would have taken the time to follow through and use her energy and enthusiasm to follow the suggestions of the true professionals in the field of home inspections and repairs. Ego and pride will bring you down every time. Being confident is great – just make sure it is not taken to extremes.

Work: **Wastes Time Talking**

We love our Flashlight co-workers when they are motivating us and encouraging the team to do well. But, when we are trying to get work accomplished the Flashlight has a tendency to talk all day every day and tell their stories. Mornings tend to be the chosen time for Flashlights to tell their stories which makes it difficult not only for them to get any work done but those within hearing distance of them as well.

I am secondary Flashlight and I must admit I am guilty of this story telling a time or two in my day. So I tell this story from a place of love and support for my fellow Flashlights.

I used to work with this woman named Connie. Connie was predominately one hundred percent Flashlight. Connie lived near me so we traveled the same route to work every day, however, she always seemed to have a different experience than I did coming to work. Things just happened to Connie that were interesting. When she got to the office she could not wait to tell her stories over and over and over as each different employee arrived. This happened several times a day. Connie was the front office receptionist. Her storytelling kept her from getting her work done. She was an excellent greeter when customers would visit the office, as she made them feel welcomed and comfortable.

Our boss came up with a plan that would help Connie tell her stories and keep her busy doing her work. We had morning sales meetings that usually did not involve Connie. He started to invite her and encouraged her to tell her story one time in front of all of us at the same time. He used Connie and her skill at motivating people to his advantage and he got her to stay busy and focused on her work while leaving the rest of us free to do our work. Our morning sales meetings started with Connie and her stories and it set the tone for the rest of the day. You see, our boss was a

Remote Control and he needed peace so he figured out a way to get what he wanted by giving Connie want she needed.

Moral to this story is that if you are a Flashlight and you emotionally need to tell your stories, be aware of how they can lead you to live in your struggle of wasting time at work, and just maybe not everyone enjoys your stories as much as you do.

Friends: Fickle and Forgetful

Living in the moment is the best way to describe Flashlights. This style also carries into their friendships. While it is easy for Flashlights to make friends, it is as hard for them to maintain their friendships. With Flashlights it is out of sight, out of mind – it could be one day, one year, or decades between contacts. Flashlights believe that if you are their friend then time doesn't matter between contacts. They expect to pick up right where they left off.

For the other personality types, this can be viewed as a personal attack. Hammers when faced with a fickle Flashlight will walk away and cut their losses. They have the need for loyalty and they will interpret a fickle friend as disloyal. The Tape Measure invests a lifetime into the few friends they have so you can imagine how they can feel hurt and wounded when they get involved with a fickle Flashlight. The Remote Control will tolerate a fickle Flashlight better than anyone since they are natural grace givers, because quite frankly it is too much energy to hold a grudge. The added bonus for the Remote Control to have a Flashlight as a friend, flighty or not, is that they will have fun because Flashlights are so much fun.

The concept of time and being on time is a big problem for Flashlights. You know we all have that friend who runs late to every event and tends to forget his or her commitments. The truth is that in the moment when the Flashlight is making the plan and commitment to you they really mean what they are saying. But an hour or a day or a week later they experience "shiny object syndrome" and completely forget about what they committed to doing with or for you. The underlying issue with the Flashlight being forgetful is their ego.

Relationship Remodeler says: "Flashlights, beware of your ego when you are not holding true or following through with your time commitments. Your healthy dose of ego has you believing whatever you need or want is more important than your commitments to others you. Flashlights are about twenty percent of the population so do the math – they are out-numbered by the other personalities that are not fickle or forgetful, and that do not struggle with ego or pride, or waste time talking. Maximize your strengths and minimize your struggles."

Strengths

The Flashlight Strengths

Emotions: Natural Curiosity

Those of us who are a Flashlight have a natural tendency to be inquisitive. While we mean no harm, this curiosity can get us in trouble.

My personal experience with this happened while I was attending a private dinner party with my husband at one of his partners' home. I had to use the ladies' room so I excused myself from the table and went to the restroom down the hall from the dining room in this house. The restroom was within ear shot of the dining room. I am in there only two minutes before my natural curiosity got the better of me. Do not ask me why I did this because I can give you no logical reason. I open a drawer in the vanity and they have one of those motion sensor cards that play music when you open it. As I open the drawer somehow the tune to "Born to be Wild" starts playing. I have been caught because I know they can probably hear it in the dining room. Sure enough I walk out and they are all laughing. The host asks, "Did you find what you were looking for?" I reply as only a quick-witted Flashlight could, "What makes you think I was looking for something? I actually was placing a tip in the drawer for excellent service and great restroom amenities. The guest towels were exquisite."

Work: Energy and Enthusiasm

When placed in the right job Flashlights can excel. They make excellent customer service representatives. Have you ever called your cable company because you just wanted to let loose and complain to someone about your cable service, only to be diffused and sidetracked by the kind and energetic customer service representative on the other end of the phone? Most likely it was a Flashlight on the other end of the phone because they have the natural ability to turn "work" into "play." You can always tell when someone is reading off a script to try and calm you down. They are not a Flashlight. Flashlights are natural and their conversations just flow easily. The high pitch and fast talk is a result of their energy and enthusiasm.

Friends: Makes Friends Easily

My husband is always amazed at how quickly and easily I make friends wherever I go. It doesn't matter where or when, but I cannot go into public without someone starting a conversation with me. I have the best experiences in Wal-Mart. It does not matter what state I am in, the most rewarding and heartfelt random conversations happen for me in Wal-Marts.

I would love to write a book on these experiences. Just the other day my husband and I were walking through our local Wal-Mart. I was trying not to make any eye contact because I was in a hurry and wanted to get what I needed and get out. As I rounded an aisle, this adorable little boy about ten years old stopped me face-to-face and said "I like your hair and your clothes. You look like a nice lady who would be fun to hang out with." I had never seen this child before this encounter. He was so adorable he wanted me to wait while he and his older brother went to find their mother in the other aisle because he said he thinks his mom would like to be my friend. I was so touched by his innocence that I waited. My husband said "It's true about your experiences at Wal-Mart." The little boy brought his mother back and she looked very frazzled and disorganized like she could have used a good friend. I introduced myself to her and paid her a compliment on her boys and their manners and obvious love for their mom because they believed she needed a friend so they went looking for one for her. Now I can see the suspicious Tape Measures reading this thinking I am naïve and they were setting me up for a scam. Not the case at all. The woman was a single mom who just lost her job and was also taking care of her sick mother and special needs child. She was on overload and just needed a friend or a complete stranger to talk to that day. My husband and I took her and her kids to McDonald's and just let her talk. We are now friends and I help her from time to time. There is something about Flashlights that have them making friends easily. Her son sensed the vibe right away. What is it they say about kids having a keen sense like dogs?

Relationship Remodeler says: "Accent the positive, eliminate the negative through self-awareness. Flashlights, be aware of how the other personalities view your actions. While your intentions may be good, not all will be impressed with your stories. So, keep them to a minimum. Stay on track and avoid too much detail. Encourage others to participate in conversations by asking their opinion. Realize that not everyone will be your best friend, especially if you do not value the time it takes to cultivate a friendship. Keep your pride and ego in check before you wreck yourself."

Flashlight Communication Adjustments
The I. A.M. Technique
(See Flashlight I. A.M. Chart on Page 86)

A – Adjustment

Limit Conversation

Flashlights need to learn to limit their conversation and allow others the opportunity to talk – even if what they have to say is more interesting and entertaining (in their minds). People who

I AM FLASHLIGHT

Identify

Adjustments

Meet in the Middle

E. V. E. N.
Method

- Learn to tone down your voice and mannerisms.
- Stay on track, and keep your stories to a minimum

Dealing with a Hammer:
- Stick to the bottom line
- Just give them bullet points
- Avoid extra details

Dealing with a Tape Measure:
- Recognize they are schedule oriented
- Be sensitive to their schedule
- They are usually single focused; do not multi task
- Be aware of their level of interest; they will tune you out

Dealing with a Remote Control:
- Encourage them
- Ask for their opinion
- Give them their 14 seconds to think about it

talk constantly eventually become a bore. Flashlights need to work on speaking only when they have something to say that people *need* to know, or that is important or vital to the situation. Remember the little boy who cried wolf? If the Flashlight isn't careful to be aware of how much they are talking, they run the risk that when they do have something important to say people have tuned them out and are not listening to them.

Whenever I am with a Flashlight who has not worked on being mindful of their communication obstacle, I am reminded of a rule my father used to have when faced with an overly zealous Flashlight. He used to say that if one is telling a story or heavy in a conversation and they are interrupted, then they should take it as a sign that the person really is not interested in hearing the story. If they urge you to continue then do so, but if they don't then you can safely assume they were not that interested anyway. This is a painful lesson for all of us who are Flashlights.

I am sure we all have a story or two about that friend who we happened to take a road trip with at one time in our life who battled for the "audience." While their stories are entertaining, they talk nonstop. When you stop to go the bathroom they will continue their story in the stall, they keep talking through the gas pumping and even when you go into the convenience store to pay and get something to drink and they are still talking. After hours of this you grow weary and pray for a few moments of silence or at least for their batteries to run out.

All of us who are Flashlights need to remember to limit our conversation. We need to be careful about overwhelming others with our words, and allow them to speak up and share their experiences with us.

Tone Down Voice

Remember, one of the visual clues for identifying the Flashlight is a loud voice. This may be a great asset if the person is a cheerleader or a public speaker in a room without a microphone. However, in most settings the loud volume is distracting and irritating and even obnoxious to others. In my experience with teaching this material the most frequent complaint of the other personalities given to the Flashlights is to tone down the volume of their voice.

My father used to have a code word for me when I was little for me to tone down my volume when I was all excited and wound up. He would just say "FM". He was making a reference to how the FM deejays used to have low, smooth, quiet speaking voices. They sounded to me like they just woke up, slow and groggy and soft. I could never really talk like that but it reminded me to talk softer and tone down the volume of my voice.

Learn to Listen

Most Flashlights think that to listen means to be quiet. The reality is, when the Flashlight appears to be listening, most likely they are just working on their next story.

It has been said that the reason people do not remember names is because they do not care enough to listen in the first place. I was certain this was not the case for me. I decided to prove this theory wrong. I planned that when I met someone new I would repeat her name within the first few minutes of the conversation. I soon found out that when I attempted to use that person's name, I could not remember it. This is not because of a poor memory – it was because of poor listening.

I have made great improvements in my listening skills. It only took a few embarrassing moments before I learned to listen better. Once I truly listened I found I was good at remembering names.

The Bible scripture James 1:19 helps me out as well and is wise advice that will help us improve our communication skills; "Everyone should be quick to listen, slow to speak and slow to become angry."

Stay on Track

A hallmark of the Flashlight's communication style is jumping from one topic to another, often without finishing any of them (guilty as charged). In Flashlight to Flashlight conversation, this is apt to be the sign two people are having a great time together.

Recently my good friend Vince and I met for lunch to catch up since we had not seen each other for a while. We both had other things we needed to do that day so our lunch was rushed. We talked quickly throughout the meal without a breath. We hugged and gave air kisses and returned to our respective cars. As I drove to my next destination, I realized that we did not finish one complete conversation. We jumped from topic to topic as one idea spurred another.

For us, this was a great meeting that was representative of how most of our visits go. But for the other personality types, this flitting conversation style can be irritating to the listener. So if you are a Flashlight, work to stay on track.

Relationship Remodeler says: "Flashlights, work on S.O.S. (shiny object syndrome). It is interpreted as a sign of disrespect to some. *More about OTHERS, less about you* should be your motto."

Let's Meet The Hammer

The Hammer

1. **Shift in Atmospheric Pressure.** I have found the best way to determine if someone is a Hammer, is not by the way they dress or the volume of their voice, but by the shift in the atmosphere when they enter a room. They never enter a room unnoticed. If they are a positive force in your life, they bring with them a sense of energy and excitement. You brace for a new adventure and see them as someone to follow. If they are a negative force in your life, they bring with them a feeling of stress and tension that could be sliced with a knife. I'm sure you can think of a few Hammers you've known just from that description alone.

2. **Likeness to the energizer bunny.** The Hammer person is highly productive and project-focused. They always have a TO DO list much longer than is humanly possible. This is the person you look at and think, "Do they ever stop?" The answer is no. Even in their sleep, they are thinking of what is next. They often find it difficult to rest, however, they do understand that sleep and rest are necessary for production so once they decide to stop for the day, they stop. Compared to the other personality types, Hammers have the highest energy level and are re-energized by activity. As long as there are things that need doing, they seem to muster the energy and effort it takes to make it happen. And then, they strongly desire credit and recognition for their achievements.

If you are not a Hammer, you may find it difficult to keep up with this person. You may find you are exhausted by all of their projects and wild ideas. Set clear boundaries with them. They need to understand what you are and are not willing to help do. They need to know how much is too much. Otherwise, they will drive you right over the edge. I assure you, nothing will seem like too much to them and they have no natural understanding of other people's limits as they do not accept them in themselves.

3. **A love for being challenged.** The Hammer is a thrill-seeker who thrives under pressure. They continuously challenge themselves to take things to the next level. Even when a new challenge is not required or necessary, they will make one up. Often, this tendency results in the Hammer making normal, routine activities and conversations more difficult. Many people struggle in relationships with a Hammer because it seems nothing is ever simple. The Hammer makes things harder and more complicated than is necessary.

   Hammers are problem fixers who are quick to jump on rescue missions or to throw out options for solving problems unless they perceive a winning solution is not possible. You see, if the Hammer can't win, they won't play.

4. **Not a democracy.** Passionate about their business, family, and causes, Hammers are natural born leaders whose basic desire in life is having their way, and they will figure out how to have it. In fact, my Hammer-entrepreneur father loves to say, "He who signs the check has the last say." Truly, they innately believe they are right and the best person for the job, often convincing themselves that they are the only one capable. Usually, this personality type is the fastest to

see the end, or big picture, which gives them tremendous decision-making ability. The problem is, they lack patience and communication skills to help everyone else see things from their perspective. They are too busy to slow down and explain. They will remove whatever or whoever is hindering progress rather than waste time helping them get on the same page. They tend to lead like dictators with an inner, or perhaps vocal, attitude that screams, "I'm driving the bus. I know where we are going and I know how to get there. Get on or get off, but I'm pulling out now."

When Hammers are living in their leadership strengths, the bus will be full of loyal and devoted followers. People are drawn to their ambition and the ability to truly get a job done and done well. However, what people won't tolerate long is being made to feel like they are stupid, replaceable, or not important. Hammers in leadership positions — which I am confident to assume are all Hammers — must remember these truths: people are more important than projects, people are not projects, and the kind of success that leaves a legacy is not possible without a team. Leaders need loyal followers. Loyal followers need honest, compassionate and thoughtful leaders who are willing to listen, ask questions and consider other points of view.

5. **Respect redefined.** Because the Hammer is so task-focused, they define respect in terms of accomplishment and the ability to make decisions. Without realizing it, most Hammers withhold admiration and respect for others until they have witnessed them succeed. Respect is earned. This explains why Hammers usurp authority and have a hard time submitting to someone who they view as incompetent or who has not rightly earned their way.

I must express a word of caution to Hammers who desire to develop into a person of unshakable character: being a person who can claim to be respectful means that even when it is difficult, you choose to show and give respect regardless of whether someone has earned it. Respect does not mean you agree, it means you treat others with the same kindness and courtesy you expect, no strings attached.

6. **Controlling or just right?** I already noted the Hammer's natural desire to have things their own way. They desire control of people, situations, finances, projects, etc. What will serve anyone with a Hammer in their life is to understand is that the Hammer's desire for control is not a choice or an attempt to drive you completely nuts, it is a need. They need control like they need oxygen. The good news is that they are designed for it and they can handle it. A Hammer, living in their strengths, has an ability unlike the other personality types to do well under extreme pressure. They can think clearly and make the right decisions under difficult circumstances without falling apart or worrying about what others will think. I hope you can recognize the emotional health; Hammers *need* loyalty from the troops, a sense of control, appreciation for service, and a sense of accomplishment.

7. **Powerful emotions.** The Hammer is often the most easy to identify when their emotional needs are not being met. They become impulsive, overbearing, impatient, and angry and then they start to "hammer" everyone and everything in their path.

E. V. E. N.
Method

Hammer

E **Emotional Need**	Loyalty, Control, Appreciation and Credit for good work
V **Visual Clues**	Energy, Body Language Function over fashion
E **Environmental Need**	Freedom, Authority, Varied activities, Difficult assignments, Opportunity for advancement
N **Natural Desire**	Control

BONUS CLUES

Method of Control	Anger
Questions they want answered	What As in "What is the bottom line?"
Motto	"My way or the highway"

Now that you have an idea of who the Hammer is, here is how you can use the E.V.E.N. method to identify them.

"E" - Emotional Needs

*Loyalty * Sense of Control * Credit for Good Work * Achievement*

Hammers are hardwired for loyalty, loyalty, loyalty, control, credit, appreciation, and achievement. Did you catch the emphasis on LOYALTY?

Loyalty

Hammers are natural born leaders and will go to the wall for those who are on our team. Our hardwiring for loyalty means that if we are leading and we go to the front lines to do battle and we happen to look back and see that any of the team has backed off, we will feel betrayed, and as a result we will, depending on our level of maturity, sever the relationship or extend grace. Not a proud moment, but in our immaturity and weakness of personality we will not only sever the relationship but we will not rest until we "hammer" the presumed disloyal person and they are destroyed. The gut reaction of most Hammers is to think it is the others person's loss. When a more mature, high functioning Hammer is faced with a situation in which they feel betrayed, they will try seeing things from the other point of view, realizing that very few people are really out to get them. These Hammers will offer grace and resolution.

Let me give you an example of my Hammer personality and the role it played in my family. I played the role of the immature

Hammer before I knew about the Temperament Theory that has saved my marriage, relationships, and my sanity. When my kids hit their teen years, they did what teens do. I wanted to kick the kids out of the house and disown them. This all stems from my deepest emotional need for loyalty. One of the biggest fears a Hammer has is having rebellious children who bring them shame and embarrassment. They internalize rebellious children as a personal failure. My husband, on the other hand, is a Remote Control who lives for peace and will take the least path of resistance and avoid controversy. His way of gaining peace was to run interference between the teenagers disobeying me. My interpretation of my kids not obeying me and my husband running interference for them left me with feelings of not being in control (which is a Hammer's natural desire) and with my emotional needs tank empty. When any personality's emotional needs tank is empty, they will do whatever they can to try and fill their tanks. The result of my emotional needs not being met and my husband's needs not being met culminated in the breakdown of my marriage.

Now that you have learned about emotional needs – those core necessities that our personalities depend on for emotional well-being and the importance of giving them to others as the process of having healthy relationships – here is what you can do for the Hammers in your life: show your loyalty to them by focusing on giving them active support. They are big picture thinkers and their focus is external; they need to see things grow and progress. The Hammers rarely ever listen to your words, but they will look for your actions. To a Hammer, action is the best indication of loyal support.

Sense of Control

Even as children the Hammer has a natural desire for control. My daughter's secondary personality is a Hammer. She was every teacher's dream student; she had every teacher's back and was very protective of the control in the classroom so everything ran smoothly. In middle school she had a teacher who was in and out of school because of breast cancer. The sensitive side of my daughter's Tape Measure primary personality had her helping out every substitute teacher for the sake of her basic education teacher who was ill. She felt sorry for her teacher so she became the self-appointed teacher's aide. However, the Hammer in her needed to be in control of the situation and at times she forgot who was really in charge of the class room. Neither the substitute teacher nor her fellow classmates stood a chance. That was until the school Principal stepped in and created a Win/Win for both my daughter and the substitute teacher. The Principal told my daughter she did not care what she chose, but she could only pick three things to be in charge of while her teacher was out. She put my daughter in control of choosing her own responsibilities for helping out. By allowing my daughter to choose her responsibilities, the Principal gave my daughter the sense that she was in control and then she was able to fulfill her natural desire of having control.

Hammers have a built-in need to be right. When they are right they will hold it over your head to make themselves feel more powerful, which translates to them as control rather than them deliberately trying to make other people feel bad. As I teach on this subject I can be pretty sure that at some point a Hammer will approach me and challenge me on a particular subject, and they will ask me if I had thought of a different perspective. Knowing the Hammer's need for control, I apply a simple sales technique that I learned years ago: I ask them what they think, giving them what they need (a sense of being in control) and then at the same time I get to keep my control. This is the "M" for *meet in the middle* where I get what I want by giving others what they need using I. A.M. technique, which we will discuss in further detail later.

Credit for Good Work

Hammers are recognized by their energy levels; they will work harder, longer and faster than anyone else. They must be at the top of the list for the person who works the hardest. If they don't get the credit for doing good work you better believe that they will go after it until someone notices.

My children were involved in musical theatre when they were younger. As you can imagine it takes a small army of people to put on a production. One of the hardest volunteer jobs to fill was that of the set builders. The set builder team usually involves about two dozen skilled carpenters and one really good organizer who is willing to take on the task. On one of the productions, the set building was more involved than normal and it required extra work and dedication from the crew leader named Bill. Bill was a Hammer and his personality was an asset to this particular production. He was harder working than the others and did an awesome job. He did however have a slight problem with his crew of Tape Measures who are hardwired to find problems by asking "why" a lot. He voiced his frustration in a joking manner to the stage manager about what he called "questioning my skills and trying to take my job over." Bill was a hard worker and could do the job of five men.

When the programs were printed up for the show his personal thank you was mistakenly left out of the program. Bill was not given a public thank you or any kind of acknowledgement. After the show was over it was noted and he was sent a handwritten but generic thank you from the director. He was apparently upset that he was not publicly given credit for his good work and his commitment to go above and beyond. When the next production came around he was cold and refused to volunteer his time. I understood his feelings were hurt and knew he needed loyalty so I made him a dinner and took it to him with my own thank you card. It was not enough for him, a case of too little too late, and he stubbornly refused to be of any help any longer and pulled his son out of the theatre group. This is a little on the extreme side, but all the same it shows how strong the emotional need for acknowledgement for hard work is for the Hammer. The lack of gratitude combined with his team's constant questioning was just too undermining for that Hammer to handle.

Relationship Remodeler says:
"Hammers, just because someone questions your way of doing something with a 'why' question does not mean they are looking to steal your credit for good work, they are just hardwired to find problems. They do not want the credit, they just want to be involved in the process without being the leader or having the spotlight on them. They just want you to acknowledge their contribution and then they will not only let you have all the public credit for good work, they will be loyal to you all day long."

Achievement

Being motivated by tasks and completing those tasks are very important to a Hammer, and not just to receive acknowledgment from others. I, for instance, can become very agitated and anxious and, let's face it, downright obnoxious when I have tasks that I need to get done and doing anything else will seem like a waste of time to me when that list is hanging over my head – no matter what the other thing is. The need for achievement runs very deep for Hammers, so much so that they have very little respect for the Remote Controls who, when living in their struggles, will not be motivated to take action on things. It is all about how many things a Hammer can do in a day. At the end of the day you can hear the Hammer reciting their accomplishments either in their heads or out loud looking for someone to give them credit for good work. My daughter who is part Hammer would have an insane amount of tasks on her list in high school. She could not do anything the easy way. If she joined one club she joined them all. To this day she supports herself 100%. She pays for her college, car, and housing, works two jobs, volunteers, and is performing in her musical at school. Her self-satisfaction comes from how many things she can do in a single day. I often tell her as the older and now wiser Hammer to slow down and enjoy her journey because the destination is overrated.

Hammers have the same 24 hours in a day that everyone else has to operate within, although their list will contain more things to do than humanly possible in a day. They will wear themselves out and push themselves to exhaustion, which only leads to them exploding on their family, friends, and co-workers. I can admit to this now and I have asked and I continue to ask my kids for forgiveness on having them overscheduled for events when they were young. I was insane when the kids were 11 and 13 years old.

I had two kids performing in two different Broadway musicals at the same time, but in two different cities. My daughter was in Los Angles and my son was in San Diego. This went on for 16 weeks. I was insane and I am certain somebody was on the receiving end of my frustration of overloading my "to do" list. I was completely driven by the task. I remember running errands at 9pm at night in Los Angeles while my daughter was in rehearsals. I drove around with a cooler in my trunk so I could grocery shop wherever I was at the time. As you have read, the Hammers need control, credit for good work, a sense of achievement, and loyalty. This 16 week road warrior trek had all of those needs met for a short time until the meltdown, and then I took a brief week off for a time out and got right back up and did it again.

Relationship Remodeler says: "Hammers, be mindful that your energy level can make more peaceful people uncomfortable and have feelings of inadequacy. Not to say you need to change your way of doing things, just remember your intentions are to get your jobs completed but the less active are judging the action, and they see it as making them look bad."

"V" - Visual Clues

Energy * Body Language * Function Over Fashion
(See Visual, Vocal, Verbal Clue Sheet on Page 182)

Hammers are not as easy to identify as the Flashlights and Tape Measures because their traits are not as obvious. While there are some clothing and body language clues of the Hammers, the best way to identify them is through the energy they bring to the room and listening to them talk.

The Hammer has a tendency to tell more than they ask, talk more than they listen, and will be blunt and to-the-point. They will make empathetic statements when they speak. Their vocal tone will be more forceful, higher volume, and faster pitched. The body language is more direct, they boldly use hands when making points, their hands are on their hips displaying impatience, and they make steady eye contact. If you shake their hand you will know it; the grip is firm and steady, very alpha dog.

Strong Energy

The Hammers do not enter a room unnoticed. If the Hammer in your life is a positive influence in your life, they will bring a sense of energy and excitement with them. If they are a negative influence in your life, they will bring energy with them, but not the good kind – they will bring stress and tension. Regardless of the effects Hammers have on you personally, they will never leave any doubt that they are currently occupying the same room as you are.

An example of the energy the Hammer brings to a room is best described by my own personal experience. My daughter could be up on the stage performing and she could feel my energy in the auditorium. When she was 11 years old and playing the role Annie in the Broadway musical of the same name, she was in the middle of a scene and she felt me as she said I was "making faces" indicating to her that I did not approve of her vocal performance. I was sitting in the 10th row of this particular theatre, and I was not in actuality "making faces." I actually had in my mono vision contacts, which meant one contact was for close vision and the other was for distance, so all I was doing was trying to get my eyes in focus and she felt my energy through her song. Wow, I am honored that my energy is noticed, but don't always assume it's a negative energy – it just may be as simple as having the wrong contacts in that day. This situation had me thinking about how strong the energy of the Hammer really can be.

Body Language

The Hammer can also be identified by their body language. They are heavy footed. The floor shakes when they walk. As I have said, I spend a lot of time on airplanes, and the flight attendants that are Hammers walk so strongly and purposefully that you can feel them coming a few seats away.

Hammers may also have a scowl on their face, not because they are angry but because they are heavy in thought about what they need to get done next. They are walking with a purpose. I have actually felt my own energy walking from the parking lot into the store when I am on a mission to get a particular task checked off of my list. I have run into people I know when I am in this mode and they have said, "Hey who are you mad at and where is the fire?"

In addition to the walk and the scowl, Hammers have three gestures that are unique to them: putting hands on hips, pointing with their fingers, and pounding with their fist. My husband who is very peaceful will always say to me, "Stop yelling at me!" I am not yelling or raising my voice, but I am talking with my hands and either pointing my finger or putting my hands on my hips while moving closer to him – I am just trying to make a point.

I do not even have to be angry to communicate with this body language. While the Tape Measures are the greatest respecter of space, the Hammers are the greatest invader of space.

Function over Fashion

Body language clues are the best way to visually identify the Hammer. If you understand that the Hammers are basically more interested in function than fashion, it is easy to see how they feel about fashion overall. The Hammer will value production and makes fashion decisions based on whether the selection will help with productivity or hinder it.

Let me explain. My husband recently had an interview with a female CEO of a manufacturing company. He said that he felt it was a bit odd that she had sneakers on with her business suit. He thought she might have had a foot injury. I asked him did she give him a tour of the manufacturing floor. He said, "Yes." I then asked, "Did she walk ahead of you or beside you?" He said she walked very fast and she was ahead of him. I said, "Nope, she did not have a foot injury. She was just a Hammer and she places a high value on productivity – wearing high heels would just slow her down." I asked several more questions about her body language. He said she talked fast and used her hands a lot to make her point. I said no test needed, she is a Hammer.

When identifying people with the Hammer personality, remember to look for people with energy who dress in a function-over-fashion manner. Also watch for the energy and body language clues: heavy-footed walk, pointing, "in your face," hands on hips and fist pounding.

Second "E" - Environmental Needs

*Freedom * Authority * Varied Activities * Difficult Assignments * Opportunity for Advancement*

Freedom

Hammers need the freedom to do what they view as the right way to do something. They do not like taking orders or being told what to do. They do a good job of setting their own boundaries. They are independent, self-sufficient and refuse to be *micromanaged*. You might even hear them use this word frequently or cite it as a core value.

Authority

They have a tendency to be dynamic leaders. They are movers and shakers. They speak with authority and conviction. You will usually find a Hammer in a position of authority – they are naturally placed in these positions because of their innate leadership skills.

Varied Activities

Hammers need to have a "dozen balls in the air at one time" for happiness. They are able to switch from one activity to the next without missing a beat. They love to improve on things. They are not afraid of new situations and love change. Just pair them with a Tape Measure to make sure their varied activities get completed and with detail.

Difficult Assignments

The challenge behind the difficult assignment keeps the Hammer happy. They thrive on opposition – tell them they can't do something and watch them go. Hammers can see the whole picture. Lean on them to get the big picture and to chart the best course. They are not easily discouraged. Appreciate that they do not take problems personally; they like the challenge.

Opportunities for Advancement

A Hammer's need for change has them always looking down the road. They have a 5-year plan and expect to get there in 3 years. They will create their own environment where they will advance. They are goal-oriented, so push them to higher production and they will excel.

Relationship Remodeler says: "Remember Hammers, it is better to motivate than to legislate."

"N" - Natural Desires

The natural desire for the Hammer is control. Hammers think that somebody needs to be in control otherwise things go terribly wrong – and this may actually be true. However, in reality we cannot control people or ALL situations, you can only control yourself. I learned through my journey of self-discovery that the more I give people what they need, the more control I actually have. It is hard to have conflict or loss of control when you are practicing the Platinum Rule. The need for control does not mean control of people but control of the situation. To be in control is the natural desire of the Hammer.

Bonus Clues

Method of Control - Anger

Hammers are the most obvious to spot when they are using their method of control, which is anger. There is no missing this; as mentioned in the visual clues you can feel the energy of the Hammer. Just being in the same space of a Hammer that is not in control will cause the hair on the back of your neck to stand up. Their emotional needs are loyalty, sense of control, appreciation, and credit for good work. The natural desire for the Hammer is control. The number one situation that will have the Hammer displaying their method of control with anger is when they feel they are losing control and feel like people will not do things their way. The biggest fear that they have is losing control of anything, losing a job, not being promoted, becoming seriously ill, having a rebellious child or unsupportive mate. They can also become agitated when they feel people are lazy and not interested in working constantly, buck their authority, and aren't loyal. Tips for you to help deal peacefully with the Hammer are to appreciate their need for decisiveness and leadership, and do not try to buck them; they will fight for you if you stand by them, so resist the urge to try and rebel when you feel controlled; they may be right in trying to control you; don't withhold appreciation; frequently express appropriate thanks and praise their hard efforts to everyone in the group. You can also simply ask them what part of their life is out of control and just listen. When they do use anger to control, show them other ways of getting people to respond. They will listen if they perceive you to be coming from a place of loyalty.

Questions The Hammer Wants Answered – "What"

The Hammer thinks in terms of *"what?"* as in What is going on here? What is the bottom line? What are we trying to accomplish? What is the agenda? Hammers are motivated by their natural desire for control (What can I do?) and the environmental need for a challenge (What is the obstacle?). The Hammer wants a piece of the action. Give them some control and it will challenge them. Hammers like choices – conflicts do not bother them. They see both as part of the territory. Remember their thought patterns of "what" and the need for challenge and control, and you will be speaking their language.

Hammer Struggles
(See Strengths and Struggles Chart on Page 43)

Emotions: Unsympathetic

Hammers will never be accused of being "warm and fuzzy." If you happen to be sick with a cold or flu, don't sit around and wait for them to bring you chicken soup. It is not going to happen. They view sickness as a sign of weakness. I am not saying if you are diagnosed with a serious illness such as cancer they would not be sympathetic because they would, maybe not as sympathetic as other personality types but they would be as sympathetic as they could for being a hard-nosed Hammer.

On the same note, a Hammer with the cold or flu most likely will not want your sympathy either. If you want to know the truth, they will be the only personality type to fake being well. Hammers do not like showing signs of weakness. If you have a personal problem and you share it with a Hammer, more than likely the attention they will give you is the solution to your problem. They will not acknowledge the feeling associated to your problem, just the solution. A Hammer parent may even say something like this to their Tape Measure child who presents them with what the child views as a personal problem because someone at school was mean to them on the playground and hurt their feelings: "First of all, this really is not a problem that we can't solve. What role did you play in this scenario?" Accountability is huge for the Hammer so they want to make sure you take responsibility if you did something to provoke the mean-spirited act. Then they might say something like "Never let a bully see you are weak or they will continue to pick on you; you have to show them you will not be pushed around. So let me give you some good solutions to stop this immediately." If you noticed, not once did the Hammer parent in this scenario show compassion to what the child may be feeling. Hammers are unsympathetic to problems because they are very task-oriented and problems are just undone tasks, so they really hear "get 'er done."

Work: May Be rude or Tactless

The above scenario with the parent Hammer is also an example of the Hammer being rude and tactless. If you understand that the Hammer is very task-oriented and not people- and relationship-oriented, then maybe you can see that when the focus is on completing their mental to do list, they can become so focused on the task that they have no concept of other people and their feelings. The adjustment that I suggest that Hammers need to make is to learn to say "please" and "thank you" more often. It also doesn't help that Hammers have a healthy ego and believe they do not need other people to help them complete those tasks on their mental to do list.

Friends: Can't Apologize

Okay, what I am about to say will most likely ruffle a few feathers of the other personality types but it is the truth so do not shoot the messenger. Realize and accept that because of their natural hardwiring to see big picture and their gift of discernment, the Hammer is *usually* right about things. Being right does not make them popular, however. If you accept this in a Hammer then you can see why apologizing often proves difficult for them.

On the flipside, the Flashlight has no problem apologizing because they are usually always in trouble and they want everyone to love them so they apologize first if it makes you love them more. The Flashlight may even apologize for something they did not even do if it gets you to be quiet and accept them more. But Hammers rarely get in trouble – and if they do, they do not realize it and that results in them not seeing the need to apologize.

If the Hammer is going to apologize it might sound something like this: "I am sorry you got upset over what I said." Kind of an apology but not, it might make you feel worse when you hear that kind of an "apology." How to apologize to each of the different personalities is a whole other book, stay tuned.

If the Hammer feels the need to apologize, they have been known to replace a verbal apology with doing something nice for you. It is not uncommon to see a Hammer husband offering to do the dishes or laundry in place of giving an apology. You might learn to accept the change of attitude as a full-on apology, just as if he was asking for forgiveness – or not. My theory is the more self-aware that you become about yourself then the easier it is to ask for a proper apology in the language you need to hear it. Just make sure you are speaking the language the listener needs to hear for effective communication.

Hammer Strengths

Emotions: Exudes Confidence

If you watch a Hammer walk into a room you will notice them because they exude confidence. It is not more noticeable than with children who by nature do things very naturally. Let me give an example. Think back to when I told you of the experiences I have in Wal-Marts.

I was in Wal-Mart on one beautiful Sunday afternoon and I was approached by this little girl who was about five years old. Her name was Bree. I felt Bree and her confidence the moment she walked into the store. For starters she was leading the pack of her family of six people. She walked in ahead of them all. I was standing in line to return something so I had a good view of her from the moment she entered the store. She was greeting everyone. I returned my item and proceeded to do some food shopping. Our eyes first met when we were standing at the deli counter. She looked at me and said, "What are you buying?" I started to tell her then she interrupted me and said she was there getting food for a picnic and asked if I wanted to join her and her family. Her mother said "I am sorry, she is just so bold." I said, "No need to apologize, she is just confident." I then asked Bree why she was asking me to attend her family picnic. Her reply was so observant and displayed the innocence of a confident, bright kid: "Well, I see you don't have a wedding ring on so you must be sad because you don't have a family to go on a picnic with today and it is such a beautiful day that my mom said we should not waste it so we should have a family picnic. We have enough food to share and I don't want you to be sad anymore." I laughed to diffuse the embarrassment of her mom. I said, "Bree, you are a very observant young lady. I am indeed not wearing my wedding ring because it is at home – I forgot to put it on this morning in a rush to get out the door to enjoy this beautiful day. I have a husband and two adult children who no longer live in my house but my husband is with me, he is just in another part of the store right now. I appreciate your offer and mostly your concern for me that you thought I might be lonely today." I assured her mom that I was not offended on any level. I appreciate a child with confidence and a compassionate heart. She reminded me a lot of my own daughter Katie at that age. I then laughed and said that she might want to invest in some Holy water and a crucifix, and I said my favorite line: "Little kids little problems, big kids big problems." I was totally joking and the mom knew it. I said to Bree, "Madam President, I will see you later."

Work: Goal-Oriented

There is a saying that if you want something done, get a busy woman to do it. Maybe the update should be if you want anything done right, get a Hammer woman to do it. I can speak for myself on this subject of a Hammer being goal-oriented. Most everything I do has a check list with a plan A, B and C. If plan A fails I have a back-up with plan B, and if all else fails I have plan C. My thought is that you can never be disappointed because one of the plans will work out with the result of your goal being met.

My son came to his father and me at the end of his eighth grade year in school and told us he wanted to play Division 1 college lacrosse. I knew nothing about college lacrosse or even how a Southern California boy would get a Division 1 college lacrosse scholarship considering lacrosse was very new to Southern California. I asked where he wanted to consider going to college to play college lacrosse. I was willing to support my son in this goal as long as he was willing to put in the effort to get his own goal. I quickly realized this was not my goal but his. I made sure it was something he really wanted to work towards before I helped him achieve his goal.

Once it was established that it was his goal, we then made it Team Heinemann goal. He told me that he wanted to go to Ohio State University to play lacrosse as one of his choices of schools. I did what was very normal for a goal-oriented, task master, big-picture-seeing Hammer. I looked Ohio State University up on the internet and found out they were not in the top twenty of NCAA College lacrosse teams. My thought was since they were not in the top twenty ranking someone would answer the phone if I called. I called and the head coach at the time answered the phone. I told him who I was and what my son wanted and could he give me any advice on how to obtain a Division 1 College lacrosse scholarship. He was more than happy to share the information with me.

The coach broke it down to three goals. He told me exactly what coaches look for when they attend recruitment camps looking for players. Armed with this information I sat down with my son and explained the amount of work that it was going to require of him to make this happen. We sat down and jointly came up with goals and bench marks for those goals. I can surely tell you that my son did all of the physical work for the following three years to obtain his Division 1 scholarship both on the field and off the field. I can also tell you that his natural born personality or that of his father would not have had the ability to pull all of this together because the big-picture-seeing of the Hammer and task-oriented factor would have made it very hard for them to set this long term goal. This was a great example of the different personalities working together for one common goal. It started with the Hammer ability to set appropriate goals for getting the job done. My son got his Division 1 lacrosse scholarship not to Ohio State University, but to Butler University. Goal set and goal achieved.

Friends: Excels in Leadership and Organization

Inside of every Hammer is a hero just waiting for a chance to show what they are made of in an emergency situation. The Hammer's quick thinking, fast action, sheer guts, and fortitude often save the day. This is good, because the Hammer's need for adventure and rescuing others require all of these attributes. Most of the time a Hammer is willing to go around, leap tall buildings, dig under, plow through, and endure pain just to fix a problem. A Hammer sees a problem and they are on it and will want to lead the efforts to get the problem solved.

Back in the day when my children were in elementary school a problem came about when the principal wanted to get rid of the annual talent show because of the amount of problems that kept coming up about the level of appropriate content that some children were displaying as talent. In typical fashion, a few bad apples will ruin the whole process for everyone. I was smart enough to know that once the talent show went away it would take an act of God to get it reinstated. The kids loved the annual talent show and looked forward to it every year. Not just my children but the majority of the students participated in the production on stage or back stage helping to put the production on. It came down to a few young ladies who decided it was appropriate to dance to Brittany Spears songs, in some parents' opinion in a "suggestive manner." I was not going to play judge or jury, I just did not want to see the talent show go away.

I rallied a few other parents to help me save the show. I made the suggestion to the principal that we have the talent show become "themed" which allowed us some control over the content. I suggested that the show have a 1900-1950s period theme. All acts must have material or music that falls into this time in history. It would also be a history learning experience. This would for sure eliminate the Brittany Spears impersonators. As you can imagine when there is change it is met with resistance. I was ok with it because I was confident in my ability to make this be a great and new experience for the kids. I lead this change with confidence and also with great organizational skills and with a crew of awesome parents who believed in my vision and creativity. The kids had a great time and more kids than ever participated in the annual talent show because they had the confidence and direction to pick a talent that made them comfortable. The staff loved it because it challenged the kids to learn something new.

The strength of my Hammer side finally got to show itself because I knew it would take a team to pull this off and I could not afford to be in my struggle as "Miss Bossy Pants" – "Miss Friendly Leader" needed to show up for this project. I had to swallow my pride a bit.

Relationship Remodeler says: "Try to show a little compassion to others when they present you with what they feel is a real problem; realize that sometimes they don't want you to fix the problem, just validate you understand how they feel. For the Remote Control and Tape Measure, one of their biggest fears is that people do not understand how they feel. If you Hammers have the need to be right, then prove them wrong, but let them know you do understand how they feel from time to time."

When it comes to apologizing, try saying the very simple words "I am sorry. I was wrong." You would be amazed by how much of an impact these four simple words will make. As Hammers you need control; say these four simple words and you will get to keep your control.

Hammer Communication Adjustments I. A.M. Technique
(See Hammer I. A.M. Sheet on Page 118)

Since the ultimate goal for the Hammer is production and accomplishment, their communication style tends to be brief and to-the-point. They are known for barking out commands with little thought for others' feelings. Perhaps this approach is practical and keeps distractions to a minimum. The Hammer should remember that communication is more than just relaying facts.

Adjustment

Be Interested in Others

Because Hammers are more focused on production and not on people, they tend to forget that people have feelings and often just view people as getting in the way of completing their tasks. Additionally, the brisk manner of many Hammers makes others apprehensive or even afraid to approach them. So one way Hammers can improve upon their communications is by being interested in others.

This can be done in several ways. One way is to actively listen to others' complete sentences – and even their entire stories. Those

I AM HAMMER

Identify

E. V. E. N.
Method

Adjustments

- Be interested in others
- Small talk at a personal level
- Ask people to do things other than demand
- Try "Will you please" versus "get me this"

Meet in
the Middle

Dealing with a Flashlight:
- Be interested in their stories
- Be appreciative of their upbeat happy attitude

Dealing with a Tape Measure:
- Allow them time to share their ideas
- They have a lot of detail
- Don't cut them off because you are a quick thinker

Dealing with a Remote Control:
- Don't shut them out
- Be patient and encourage them
- Learn to listen because they talk slower

who are Hammers are usually quick thinkers and processors, often knowing what other people are trying to say long before it has even been said. Because Hammers are looking for the bottom line or bullet point as I say, they have a tendency to cut people off in mid- sentence by saying something like "Yeah, yeah, I got it." In the fast-paced business world this style of communication may serve as an effective way to relay information to co-workers or employees. But for the rest of the world, the "get to the point" approach shuts people down and limits further communication.

Cultivate Small Talk

The old saying about stopping to smell the roses is great advice for the Hammers. Because their focus on work and completing tasks takes up all their time and energy, Hammers do not typically take the time they should to invest in others. Because of this, they have limited ability to converse on topics of interest to others and often find small talk to be a waste of time.

A friend of mine told me how disappointed she was that her mother's focus on work was so consuming that there was little time for just a simple conversation. She thought she would take up tennis so she could find a common interest with her mother who used to play tennis – yet her mother showed no interest in joining her. Her mother was also a gourmet cook so she thought she would ask her mother to teach her how to cook – however, her mother would cancel one lesson after another. Over the years, their conversations had dwindled to the perfunctory telephone calls on birthdays.

Hammers need to broaden their areas of interest in order to communicate with others. This might include watching a little more TV, taking up a sport, spending more time outdoors, or taking up a hobby – anything that will expose them to something different.

If you are a Hammer, broaden your horizons. You will find that you not only have more interests, but you are also more approachable.

Ask Rather Than Demand

Remember your mother teaching you to use the magic words when requesting something? I bet they were "please" and "thank you." In the bottom-line communication style for the Hammer, these niceties are often forgotten. The reality is that by not using the word "please" the words of the Hammer are often interpreted as a command that ensures that the other personalities will use their power to "opt out." This often builds resentment in people toward the Hammer personality type.

Often in my group teachings on the personalities I will divide the participants into small groups and ask them to make a list of the things they would change about the other personalities (Kind of a trick question because I am sure by now you have figured out that you cannot change people, but you can change your approach to them). The most common thing that others wish they could change about the Hammer personality is the way in which they demand or command things. They just want to hear those simple but oh-so-powerful words from the Hammer – "please" and "thank you." Hammers, if you want to be in control and have power, then learn to say the powerful words "please" and "thank you" and adjust your tone to ask rather than demand.

Let me give you an example of this situation.

As I am writing this book children have been back to school for about two months. I was standing in line at one of my favorite discount big box stores to return something. The lady in front of me in line was definitely a Hammer. As I have said before, you will feel their energy – if they are a positive influence then you feel positive energy, and if they are negative influence you will feel negative energy. Let's just say that I – as well as everyone else around her – felt her negative energy as she approached the clerk behind the counter. The Hammer was returning her son's backpack because after about forty-five days the zipper on this brand name backpack broke and the seams were coming apart. She was asking for a refund from the clerk. The clerk responded by telling her she did not think they could refund her money because the store policy was thirty days for a refund. Angered because such an obviously defective backpack ought to earn a full refund, this Hammer woman said, "Oh, but you will refund my money. I need to speak to YOUR manager." The manger appeared and instructed the clerk to refund the lady's money. The clerk was noticeably unfriendly during the rest of the transaction even though the lady tried to be more light-hearted. The clerk was not having any part of it.

I stood there trying very hard not to take one of my business cards out and hand it to the lady with some smart comment like "Here, let me teach you how you can get more flies with sugar than with vinegar" or "I can help you in the future to learn how to get what you want by giving others what they need" or my personal favorite, "Learn how to make things right by getting E.V.E.N." I did refrain because I knew that it was the Hammer in me that wanted to be in control of the situation, and I know – because I am one – that the last thing that Hammer lady was going to do was listen to anyone because her behavior (her action) was what everyone in line was judging her on. She was judging herself on her intentions (to get a refund on a defective backpack) and she did not see herself or her actions the way the rest of us standing in line did on that day. I am confident that this lady has a lot of strife and unhappiness in her personal relationships. As a Hammer she has too much pride to learn something new, and she is unaware of the power of her demanding ways.

In summary, Hammers believe that the time, effort and energy it takes to relate to people does not help the bottom line. However, if they truly want to be more productive, they will recognize that the nonproductive time it takes to ask questions, to listen and to say a heart-felt "thank you" will make them more productive in the long run.

Relationship Remodeler says: "When communicating with others, Hammers need to remember the magic words our mothers taught us and be mindful of the tone of our voices as well. A good verse to remember as Hammers is Proverbs 16:24, 'Kind words are like honey – enjoyable and healthful' (TLB)."

Let's Meet The Tape Measure

The Tape Measure

1. **Admirable reservation.** Tape Measures are quiet, controlled, polite, detailed and introverted. They generally dress in a modest/conservative style and are neatly groomed, starched, and sprayed. Not only do they have naturally quiet voices, they also only speak and share on a need-to-know basis. They value privacy and are content to keep to themselves. Unlike the Flashlight, they do not feel the need to share and expose all of their personal information and thoughts.

2. **Attention to detail.** It seems the Tape Measure thinks of everything. These intellectuals help the group see long-term goals. They are the most organized of all the personality types, having a place for everything and keeping everything in its place. They know when someone has touched their belongings. Tape Measures are great planners and live by their schedules, incorporating all important and minor details into their overall strategies. They like using lists, charts, and graphs as guides. I admire their ability to catch and prevent mistakes; however, too much attention to detail can become overwhelming to others and delay progress. It is important for the Tape Measure to learn to overlook items that may not be necessary for overall success.

3. **Attempts at perfection.** A Tape Measure's natural desire in life and motivation for doing most everything is to

attain perfection. Whether it is with relationships, work projects, or domestic duties, the Tape Measure aims to do things the right way. They have very high standards and expectations for most everything. They have a desire to work alone. After all, someone else will likely mess up the plan or do something the wrong way. They have lists of unwritten rules that you must measure up to. Unrealistic expectations can make the Tape Measure very hard to please and add intense pressure to relationships. When things go imperfectly, the Tape Measure becomes the victim. This can make it very difficult to work alongside a Tape Measure personality type if you are not one.

4. **Admiration for magnificence.** Because the Tape Measure is so detail-oriented, they often have a deep appreciation for nature and its beauty. Many Tape Measures are highly talented and creative, and often artistic or musical. They are high achievers because of their self-discipline and desire for perfection. Generally, they strive to perfect their craft for the love of the art, rather than for the applause of an audience or to perform. Intense introspection may cause them to retreat or seem off in another world as they ponder and dream about ideals.

5. **Attitude of compassion.** Tape Measures are naturally deeply concerned for others. They are very sensitive and often moved to tears with compassion. They are faithful and devoted companions, although they generally hold back affection and are insecure in social environments. While they may feel for others, they rarely share those feelings and hesitate to reach out and take action, fearing they will not do the right thing and embarrass themselves.

6. **Assumption in relationships.** As I already noted before, Tape Measures desire perfection and that also applies to relationships. They exercise great caution in making friends because they are natural skeptics who are suspicious of the intentions of others. In relationships, Tape Measures are often seen as moody or depressed because they carry a dark cloud of disappointment when they do not agree with the actions or decisions of others. If a Tape Measure does not make a conscious decision to be positive, they may become critical, antagonistic, and vengeful. They never forget an offense.

7. **Altering emotions.** Like the Flashlight, the Tape Measure is emotional. However, while the Flashlight has extremely high highs and rare lows which are usually short-lived, the Tape Measure has extremely low lows and rare highs which are usually short-lived. To obtain and maintain emotional health, Tape Measures *need* sensitivity and understanding, support when down, space and times of silence – meaning no people. I have found that the best thing you can do for the Tape Measures in your life, if you are not a Tape Measure, is to slow down, sit down and shut up. Allow them to be immersed in their pain; don't ignore them, but don't try to jolly them up.

E. V. E. N. Method

Tape Measure

E **Emotional Need**	Sensitivity, Support, Space & Silence
V **Visual Clues**	Quiet, Closed, Neat and Tidy
E **Environmental Need**	Clearly defined tasks and explanations, Sufficient time and resources to accomplish tasks, Team participation, Limited risks, Planning and precision.
N **Natural Desire**	Perfection

BONUS CLUES

Method of Control	Mood Swings
Questions they want answered	Why As in "Why are we doing this?"
Motto	"Houston, We Have a Problem"

"E" – Emotional Needs

*Sensitivity * Support * Space * Silence*

Tape Measures are naturally hardwired with the need for those around them to be sensitive to their feelings. Their biggest fear is that people do not understand what they are feeling or what they are going through. They need to be understood and supported and they need space to feel their pain. Their heads become foggy when there is too much noise, they need quiet time to feel peace with themselves and what's going on in the world around them.

Sensitivity

I made the big mistake of not giving my daughter the sensitivity she needed as a Tape Measure. Being true to my Hammer nature and being a big picture thinker with problem-solving skills, then factor in my need for people to take accountability, I blew it big time. My daughter would come to me with a problem and I would listen, but I wasn't just hearing her. I was busy trying to formulate a solution for her "perceived problem." I say perceived because to me it was really never a problem, because I could see how to solve it. Hammers will focus 90% on the solution and only 10% on the problem. This is the exact opposite for Tape Measures. They are the ones who are recognized by Hammers as the Eyores of life. There used to be a cartoon character in the Flintstones series called "Schlep Rock" who walked around saying "wowsy wowsy woe." He had a black cloud over his head. He was the poster child for a Tape Measure that has taken their strength of recognizing problems to the extreme and focusing just on the problem and not the solution. This is due to the little hidden secrets that Tape

Measures do not want you to know. Their biggest fear is nobody understands what they are going through.

This is important enough to repeat again. My daughter's need was for me to be sensitive to what she was feeling and what she was going through. She also needed for me to be sensitive to the timing in which I gave my advice. Timing is everything with the Tape Measure. Think through their thoughts and feelings before you speak. I had no idea of this need for her. I only knew what I needed in that particular situation and I gave her what I needed: action. I would have needed to take action and solve the problem and I would need to be cheered up (Flashlight need) with some shopping or ice cream. Mistake number one, I did not practice the Platinum Rule of giving her what she needed. Tape Measures do not need to be cheered up or have their problem solved, they need a good ear and some sensitivity for what they are feeling. If you make the mistake of trying to minimize the problem or cheer them up, be prepared for them to control you with a mood swing and become quiet and shut down. Do not do what I did – I repeat, *do not do this*. When she finally felt like I had suffered enough with her silent treatment and she told me what her problem was, I responded with, "That doesn't seem to be such a big deal, but more importantly what role did you play in this issue, and what lesson can you learn from this situation?" Oh my, what I know now. I was constantly giving her what I needed instead of what she needed. She eventually shut down and would not tell me what was bothering her. I cannot stress this point nough: when one's emotional needs tank is empty, they will find her ways to get it filled and it usually is not healthy.

ˉ you are the Tape Measure and your friend, or co-worker ite is trying to be helpful by asking what is wrong, answer them honestly. Flashlights and Hammers living in their strengths will understand and adjust their approach so that you will know they care. However, someone who does not know about the personality languages will give up and not even bother to ask the next time. Tape Measures are very sensitive to not only their emotional needs but that of others. Hammers need to give them a break and learn from them on how to be more sensitive.

Relationship Remodeler says: "When you are faced with a constant complainer, give them what they need – sensitivity. Try saying this the next time: 'I am so sorry you are going through this, it must make you feel (fill in the blank).' They do not want the problem solved, they just want you to be sensitive toward them. Eventually when you give them sensitivity they will stop the complaining; the complaining is the result of you not giving them sensitivity. Be more sensitive when dealing with the Tape Measures in your life. They are deep and sensitive, feeling individuals. They can and will take on others' pain so be sensitive to their feelings."

Support

In my class for becoming a Certified Personality Trait Educator our instructor told us to think of the Tape Measure as a bridge. She said without the support of people who care, the Tape Measures will feel let down and fall apart.

I did do this with some amount of success with both my husband and daughter, who both share the Tape Measure personality trait, over the years. In regards to my husband I supported him and his career over the years. I could have easily taken center stage when it came to being around his co-workers, but I did not; I put the spot light on him and his needs, and supported him in whatever it took to build his career. I have moved nineteen times in 31 years of marriage to support his career. I did this all with the purpose of supporting him. I did this for my daughter and her singing and acting career. I spent many years driving her to vocal lessons an hour and a half one way once a week, not to mention the tours she did, including the Nashville scene for a recording contract. I also supported my son in his journey toward getting his Division 1 lacrosse scholarship. It was all my efforts to show them I supported them in their goals and dreams. They all know by my actions that I supported them and have become very proud of them.

There is not a lot I did to give my daughter her emotional needs because I really did not understand her or the personality language she needed me to speak, but support is one of her needs I did give to her. I am still giving her support on her career choice, while I am not personally happy about her choice to forgo her singing career for a teaching credential. I am, however, supporting her choice. I am not going to lie, this is very hard for me in my Hammer personality to support her choice. My wisdom and discernment thinks something different, but I will give her what she needs – my support. Giving her support doesn't mean have to give up on dreaming that she goes back to her singing er, it just means I cannot take action on it.

Space

Tape Measure children are easy to identify. They are the ones who do not like for their things to be touched and they themselves do not like to be touched. Hugs are not their thing, giving them or receiving them. The worst torture you could do to a Tape Measure child is to have them share a room with their Flashlight or Remote Control sibling.

My daughter had a stage manager once who was a Tape Measure, which is a good fit for that job because of the detail and accuracy needed. This stage manager had this issue with the actors (Flashlights) who insisted on hugging everyone whether they were coming or going. He would put his hand up like you do when you are trying to stop someone, but his palm was pointed inches from his face. He said, "You are here," then he would flip the hand over and push it away from his face and say "and I need you there." He was setting his space boundaries. This space issue is one of the places that Tape Measures will have unwritten rules about how they need their space respected. Just know that if the Tape Measures in your life have problems and they are quiet and pulling away from you, don't take it personally. They just need their space to get in touch with what they are feeling.

Relationship Remodeler says: "Flashlights do not take it as a personal rejection if a Tape Measure shuts you out when they are dealing with something personal. They do not have your passion for sharing your most private struggles, where you need to talk things out they do not. Give them their space and do not try to cheer them up."

Silence

The saying "silence is golden" was probably coined by a Tape Measure. They need silence – too much noise or talk makes them uptight. If you are a Flashlight, have you ever been shushed for talking too loud or too much? Most likely you were shushed by a Tape Measure. My son is partially a Flashlight so he tends to talk more than the average person, and when telling a story the volume of his voice gets louder as the story gets longer. My daughter has shushed her brother a time or two.

The worst thing I remember as a child being raised by a Tape Measure father was our drive to school in the morning. Silence was a must – no talking. My dad called it "collecting his thoughts." He told me I should try it, as it was a good habit to get into for one to have a perfectly productive day. I said, "Why would anyone have to collect their thoughts? Mine are always right here." I would point to the front of my head. As a Hammer/Flashlight blend, I always have thoughts in my head. The problem is that they never go anywhere – they are always there. The brain does not shut off, so I did not understand the concept of collecting my thoughts. I now understand my dad was just doing what came naturally to him, playing the silence.

My husband is not much of a talker and getting him to engage in a conversation for any length of time is like pulling teeth. So vhen I need to have an in-depth conversation and do a lot of aring, I call my other Flashlight friends. After 31 years I have ned to adapt and look on the bright side. If Tape Measures silence, then great – it is less complaining I need to hear! lding.

"V" – Visual Clues

Quiet * Perfect * Closed * Neat and Tidy
(See Visual, Vocal, Verbal Clue Sheet on Page 182)

Tape Measures have the second most obvious visual clues to identify them. If you look on the basic personality chart you will notice that the Flashlight and Tape Measure are diagonal from each other, which make them polar opposites. The Flashlight is loud, open and cluttered; the Tape Measure is quiet, closed, and neat and tidy.

Quiet and Perfect

The Tape Measure is quiet, and that quiet manifests itself most noticeably in a quiet voice. You probably have a Tape Measure in your life that when you are on the phone with them you are able to hear them fine in the beginning of the conversation, but as time goes on their voice trails off as they become comfortable. Where the Flashlights have naturally loud voices, the Tape Measure is just the opposite and they have to work at projecting their voice.

Tape Measures have a very low-volume, slow speech, and a monotone delivery. They will show fewer facial expressions and will not touch you when speaking. In fact, they do the opposite as they have personal space issues. Their stories will be more fact- and task-oriented, have limited to no personal sharing, be very focused, and have a very proper delivery.

The Tape Measure also likes quiet, subtle colors like black, white or gray. They are drawn to more traditional, classic styles. Everything about their looks will say "I am perfect." I was at the dry cleaner's one day and this woman was wearing a black turtle neck with a fresh pair of perfectly pressed khakis and a pair of loafers. She was giving instructions to the proprietor on exactly how to press the other pair of khakis she was bringing in; she was determined to get her pockets pressed so everything was just perfect. She kept using the word perfect to describe what she wanted. This was the poster child for all things saying, "Hey, I am a Tape Measure."

Closed

As much as the Flashlights are open, Tape Measures are closed. They fully embrace the adage that "silence is golden" and they keep their mouths shut. They will often become annoyed with the Flashlight who talks too much and tells too many stories. I think that in a previous life most Tape Measures were CIA agents and took the oath of "need to know." They are hard to get to know and divulge very little personal information about themselves. They also have closed body language; you will not find them giving hugs, and I think I have figured out why. Remember the lady who wanted her Khakis starched and pressed a particular way? I believe that the Tape Measure does not want to be hugged because it might wrinkle them.

Neat and Tidy

The personal space of the Tape Measure is, well, perfect, neat, and tidy. They like everything in their home, car, or office to be in perfect order. Tape Measures do not multitask well, for they find it hard to do anything right when too many things are going on at the same time. They cannot work in a messy, cluttered environment.

I have a friend that has a walk-in pantry in her kitchen. She has all of her spices removed from their original containers and they are labeled with a label maker and they are color coded by sweet or savory. She also has all of her canned goods alphabetized. Her pantry looks like a show case where one would display their trophies and awards. She is also the friend who has kitchen cabinets with glass door fronts. She has given a new meaning to neat and tidy.

Second "E" – Environmental Needs

*Clearly-Defined Tasks and Explanations * Sufficient Time and Resources to Accomplish Tasks * Team Participation * Limited Risks * Assignments that Require Planning and Precision*

Clearly Defined Tasks and Explanation

Tape Measures can be afraid to start a project if they do not have the steps clearly defined in advance. If you give these needs to them, the Tape Measure will sacrifice for you or the company. They need to finish the task – they do not like being set up to fail, so they will ask a million questions to make sure they have it "perfect." They will challenge you if the task is not clearly defined.

Sufficient Time and Resources to Accomplish Task

Never put a Tape Measure in a situation where there is not enough time to complete a task. They need to do the best job they can and they do not rush through tasks; they will become depressed if they do not have the time or resources to finish the job. Tape Measures need to be aware of setting their goals too high, especially when time is not on their side. They do not need to be the first one done, just the one who has done the job better and more accurately than others.

Team Participation

While Tape Measures do not need to be the team leader, they do, however, like team participation. They are the ones you want on your team, because they are hardwired to see potential problems. They can also be very creative, detailed, and schedule-oriented. When Tape Measures feel comfortable and validated they will be loyal to you until their death. Tape Measures are hardworking team players if you can wade through their critical questions and sometimes critical judgments.

Limited Risks

Being very cautious, careful, and calculating, the Tape Measure will calculate how many risks are involved before they commit to taking on new tasks. Tape Measures usually find what they like and stick to it. Being consistent, they enjoy being in their comfort zone. They are able to limit their risks when they have clearly defined expectations, sufficient time and proper resources to complete the task. This is all part of the environmental needs that the Tape Measure must have in place for success.

Assignments that Require Planning and Precision

Since the Tape Measures are extremely conscientious they can stay on track with a project long after others have given up. For leisure, they like to do jigsaw and crossword puzzles because they can see how things fall into place with precision. They have an inventor's mind and instinct because of their environmental need for planning and precision. The bigger the need for detail, the happier they will be.

Relationship Remodeler says: "You must have imperfections to know what perfection really is. You should strive for excellence not perfection. We do not live in a perfect world. There is only one perfect place and that is Heaven."

"N" – Natural Desire

The Tape Measure's natural desire is perfection, not just for themselves but also for others to be perfect. I think striving to do a good job is in and of itself a great and noble gesture, but when you get so caught up in the need for everything to be perfect that you project your need for perfection on others, you need to be very careful. This natural desire can be a double-edged sword when taken too far. Nobody and no one thing is perfect. Perfection does not really exist. I have a saying that "You have to have imperfection to have perfection." The need for perfection is very strong for the Tape Measure and it is usually their cause of frustration when they cannot get others to buy into the expectation that all things need to be done right and perfectly. Their motto is "A job worth doing is worth doing right and perfectly."

Bonus Clues

Method of Control – Mood Swing

Tape Measures will become depressed when their natural desire for perfection and for things to be done right is not met and life is out of order. They also will be unhappy when their standards are not met and no one seems to care or understand what they are going through, or if they make a mistake. They will spend too much time on preparation, are too focused on detail, remember negatives and are suspicious of others. Their method of control is mood swings. Tape Measures' emotional needs of space, silence, sensitivity support and a sense of stability have them being the most emotional of the personalities. If you live with a Tape Measure you know they control frequently with their mood swings. Have you ever heard of the expression "walking on egg shells around this person"? Chances are they are referring to a Tape Measure. If you happen to be a person who is forgetful, late, disorganized, superficial, prevaricating and unpredictable, you have been on the receiving end of a Tape Measure using their method of control with a mood swing. You can help a Tape Measure by appreciating their need for high standards and their pursuit of excellence. Be aware of easily hurt feelings, and don't joke around – they need understanding. They will sacrifice for you, so let them know you support them. Give them time and space to complete their job; they want to do it right. Work at giving them a quiet space. When they get depressed because they feel like no one understands them, ask them to explain; then really listen and ask questions. When they pull one of their mood swings on you, don't buy into the drama or depression; instead, ask how to solve the problem.

Questions The Tape Measure Wants Answered – "Why"

The Tape Measure thinks in terms of *"why?"* Why are we doing this? Why are we working on this job? Why was I assigned this task? Why am I reading this book? They are motivated by this environmental need of quality answered (Why is this happening?) and correctness (Why are we doing it this way?). It is better to tell a Tape Measure that you do not know the answer than to fake it. Better yet, tell them you will do some research and get back to him later when you find a satisfactory answer. Then do your homework. A Tape Measure will respect you, admire your diligence, and help you complete your task in style. Remember the thought pattern of "why" and the environmental need for "quality answers" and "correctness" and you will be speaking their language.

Tape Measure Struggles
(See Strengths and Struggles Chart on Page 43)

Work: Spends Too Much Time Planning and is Hard to Please

The Tape Measure is a perfectionist that can make even the simplest of projects into a big task. This is most evident with the Tape Measure entrepreneur. While they may have a brilliant idea, it may still be left on the drawing board because they cannot have things perfect enough for them to launch their product. They can also be difficult to work with; they are so hard to please because of the unwritten rules they have for things and people to be perfect.

There is a Tape Measure in one of my networking groups who has not gotten her website up and running because she cannot decide on a photo of herself. She has been to three different photographers to get that one perfect picture. She has an awesome business that she is denying to the world because she cannot decide on the perfect picture, plus she has put her entire team on hold because she will not make a decision on a simple picture. Do not get me started on how much planning she has done on her website with regards to content, shopping cart, sales copy etc., but she will not launch her site until it is perfect. I guess she has never heard of the business theory "build the plane as you fly it."

Emotions: Can be Moody or Depressed

With their thoughtful and sensitive nature, Tape Measures can be easily hurt. Always wanting life to be perfect, they are frequently let down by the reality of an imperfect world. If you are married to a Tape Measure, it is important to recognize the things that will make your spouse feel sad. As you come to understand their personality, you can give them the support as they experience their mood swings or depression.

If you work with a Tape Measure realize they have a tendency to become depressed or moody over imperfections and will control by their mood swings. Affirm their mood; don't try and change it but do ask them to limit their acting out in the workplace.

Your Tape Measure child's deep, thoughtful and analytical nature will take him or her far, but taken to the extreme, these traits can cause the Tape Measure to brood over problems and constantly criticize everyone and everything that doesn't meet a perfect standard. They will control through mood swings when life becomes too much for them.

Friends: Suspicious of People

When I first moved to Philadelphia back in 1990 it was very hard and lonely for me. I had a brand new baby and no family.

My only friends were the neighborhood kids who were what used to be called latch key kids. They had nobody to come home to after school so most days they would come over to my house for company. I appreciated it because I needed a break from being home all day by myself with a brand new baby and no human contact all day. The girls loved the attention and got to feel important because they could practice learning how to be a babysitter.

One day they came over and I had to tell them that we were going to be on vacation for the next few weeks so they would not be able to come over and visit. My husband who is a secondary Tape Measure had to let me know that I was not that smart to be telling these neighborhood girls that we were not going to be home for two weeks. He said while I was at it, why didn't I just give them our house key so they could let themselves in to use our house as party central. I said, "Come on they are kids." He said, "But you don't know, maybe they have older friends who they will try to impress by letting our empty house act as their new hang out." He is simply suspicious of people with no merit to his concern.

Relationship Remodeler says: "Tape Measures, your problem isn't your problem – it's your attitude toward your problem. Your attitude affects your altitude. Sometimes when you are suspicious of people, you really are giving them too much credit for thinking or doing something that in reality most people aren't that creative to do or say whatever you think they have."

Tape Measure Strengths

Emotions: Sensitivity to Others

Of all of the personalities, Tape Measures feel the full spectrum of emotions. This ability to feel emotions makes them perfect sympathizers to others' pain and problems. Unlike the Hammers, who feel the need to fix the situation, the Tape Measure will sit and listen quietly to you and then sympathize with your struggle. This acute sensitivity can be both a benefit and a disadvantage, as Tape Measures can often misunderstand that many of the emotions they are feeling are "borrowed" and not their own. It may take some time for them to figure out how to live with this gifting.

This gift of sensitivity gives Tape Measures the ability to decipher the smallest differences in taste, textures, misspelled words, improper grammar, mathematical stress loads, and the details of legal fine print. When Tape Measures apply these emotions to the arts, masterpieces are born. Taken to a deeper level, this ability to be sensitive allows Tape Measures to communicate in a metaphor, which may be lost on the shallowness of the Flashlight or the bottom line of the Hammer. No other personality type has produced more brilliant artisans and poets.

Work: Likes Charts, Graphs, and Lists

The Tape Measure is often predisposed toward a love of charts, lists and graphs. One day I was at my friend Carla's house and I saw all of these yellow Post-It notes all over her kitchen pantry door. Each Post-It note contained one item. I asked her what all of these notes were about, and she replied, "They are things waiting to get on my master grocery list." I said, "Why don't you just have one list where you put all of these items?" She said, "Because I have to organize my master list by aisle." It seemed logical when she explained it, but that method would not have entered my mind.

Friends: Deep Concern for other People

If you ever have to have bad news delivered to you it might serve you well to have it delivered in the presence of a Tape Measure. Let me give you an example. I was sitting in the hospital waiting room one day when a woman received some rather sad news about her husband and his biopsy. The doctor was an obvious Hammer because of his delivery of the sad news. He just gave her the facts and said "He has about a 2 percent chance that he will live another 5 years." This just saddened the woman who was beginning to cry about the possibility that her husband would not be around to see their only son graduate college. One nurse tried to help her solve the problem by presenting the options while the receptionist just allowed the woman to cry and provided her with tissues and comfort until she calmed down. The woman just needed for someone to feel her pain and not try and solve the problem. The receptionist was a great Tape Measure and was operating in her strength that day.

Tape Measure Communication Adjustments
I. A.M. Technique
(See Tape Measure I. A.M. Sheet on Page 144)

For those of you who are Tape Measures whose natural desire is for perfection, please remember that being perfect and wanting "things" perfect are two different animals, so to speak. Being perfect is impossible, but desiring that "things" be perfect isn't a bad quality as long as you don't take it to extremes. While there

I AM TAPE MEASURE 📷

Identify

E. V. E. N.
Method

Adjustments

- Lighten up
- Don't take life that serious
- Enter into conversations
- Don't allow Flashlights & Hammers to dominate

Meet in the Middle

Dealing with a Flashlight:
- Respond openly to their humor
- Their stories are funny so laugh openly
- Compliment them often, they thrive on them
- When compliments are given they will thrive

Dealing with a Hammer:
- Don't bog them down with details
- Give them bottom line bullet points

Dealing with a Remote Control:
- Remember by nature they see negative first
- Keep things positive

may be many aspects of this personality type that are perfect, there are some areas in which the Tape Measure can improve – especially in the area of communication.

A - Adjustments

Lighten up

The Tape Measure is the opposite of the Flashlight. While the Flashlight needs to learn to listen, listening is one of the strengths of the Tape Measure. The Flashlight is naturally funny, while the Tape Measure has to work at adding humor to their communication – lighten up.

It is true that Tape Measures are naturally hardwired to see problems which, used in the right context, can be their biggest asset. However, they are best received when they realize not everyone likes to hear about problems.

For example, a Flashlight does not like to hear about problems. They live for fun and hearing about a problem does not make things fun for them. Their emotional need is for acceptance and approval, so when a Tape Measure comes along and points out a problem, the Flashlight will hear that "I am the problem, I am wrong for being who I am, I did something wrong." Because the Flashlight is naturally hardwired to be more focused internally, they will internalize everything said to them, whether it is good, bad or in-between. If the Tape Measure wants to be heard by the Flashlight, they must be mindful of how they present the problem to the Flashlight. If the Tape Measure takes a lighter approach to presenting the problem and avoids stating it in a context that the Flashlight takes as personal then the Flashlight is open to hearing the problem.

The same principal applies to adjusting your approach to the Remote Control. It is the old saying that "It's not what you say but how you say it." Just lighten up, Tape Measures, and realize that not every problem you see needs to be heard by everyone. Your need is for perfection, which is not the case for the other three personality types.

As a Hammer, I personally love to work with Tape Measures now that I understand that they are naturally hardwired to see problems because of their natural desire for perfection. I used to think that they were just troublemakers who enjoyed trying to take the spotlight when working in a group, and who enjoyed being in the center of drama caused by them pointing out all problems. I understand now that Tape Measures usually do not see the bigger picture like Hammers do, however; they see the detail and have the skill to point out things that have the potential to be bigger problems down the road. I have a few rules now when dealing with Tape Measures so the fault-finding and problem-finding does not get out of control. One: If this problem won't matter in four weeks, then do not point it out. Two: Do not criticize or point out a problem without a solution. Three: Be mindful of the personality type that you are pointing out the problem to and speak their language so you increase the odds that they are effectively listening to you. In general, Tape Measures need to lighten up and realize that you are the only one needing perfection.

Enter into the Conversation

Since the Tape Measures are natural listeners, not talkers, they must work to participate in the conversation. It is very easy for Tape Measures to feel hurt that no one cares enough to ask what they think or how they are feeling. While it is true that those of us who are not naturally sensitive and caring like the Tape Measure need to learn to be more sensitive, Tape Measures also need to take the responsibility to enter into the conversation. From my experience, when the Tape Measure is quiet during a conversation it just gives them more time to be critical in their heads. When speaking, it allows for less time of thinking about the problem they may or may not see.

Think Positively

The natural desire of the Tape Measure is perfection. Because these individuals desire perfection in themselves, they expect it from others. This natural tendency also allows them to see all of the flaws in people and programs – which make them prone to being critical.

If you are a Tape Measure, you should work on thinking positively. It does not come naturally. My daughter told me that she keeps Ephesians 4:29 in mind daily: "Do not let any unwholesome talk come out of your mouths but only what is helpful for building others up according to their needs, that it may benefit those who listen." Work on offering praise and encouragement to others, rather than criticism. Make an effort to watch for opportunities to build others up and give unqualified praise; you are discouraging other personalities from even trying.

I have a couple that I coach, and she is a Flashlight/Remote Control while her husband is a Tape Measure/Hammer. They just moved to a new home. The husband is in the military and would be joining her in a few weeks in their new home. I suggested to her that as a token of good will she might unpack his desk items and have his new office all set up for him before he got home since I understood the mind of the task master Tape Measure/

Hammer personality. I knew he would be grateful to have his office ready to go so he could hit the ground running. She said to me "I would not even attempt to unpack his things. I wouldn't do it right for him anyway. He would just point out all of the things I did wrong." Over the years her Tape Measure husband had already trained her to not do kind things for him – for fear she would not do it right.

She pointed out to me something I already knew and understood all too well about the Tape Measure personality. Tape Measures feel that endorsing what they feel is substandard behavior in others will signal that a particular behavior or work level is acceptable, when really change should be made. However, if you are a Tape Measure, you need to realize that others are more likely to change or improve with positive reinforcement than with criticism.

Relationship Remodeler says: "Tape Measures, if you can't say something nice to or about someone, don't say anything at all. At a minimum, adjust your approach to meet the needs of the person on the receiving end."

Let's Meet The Remote Control

The Remote Control

1. **The Beauty Queen.** Have you ever seen a caricature of a beauty queen? Her perfectly proportioned features do not create a funny and entertaining cartoon. That is because there is nothing extreme about her to accentuate. I call the Remote Control the beauty queen, because in the same way, there is nothing *extreme* about them. These chameleon-like, go-with-the-flow types are easy to get along with and pleasant to have around. Often referred to as the "green grass," they fill in the missing or sparse places where the other personalities lack.

2. **Favorite household item - The Recliner.** Remote Controls are often found in a relaxed or reclined body position and have the lowest energy level of all. They move at a slower pace than the other personality types and don't tend to get in a hurry... ever. Their motto is: "Why stand when you can sit, and why sit when you can lie down?" If you'd like to test the theory, take a Remote Control to a really crowded restaurant where people are standing in line. If the wait is going to be more than 30 or 40 minutes and they can see that they are not going to be able to sit down, they will want to go somewhere else – just ask. Or, should they insist on staying because they don't want to risk upsetting you, they will amuse you with the creative places they will locate to plop down.

If you are not a Remote Control, you may find it difficult to slow to this person's easy and relaxed pace. You may find you are irritated by their casual, effortless style. Try to relax and take the opportunity to develop patience. But, for the sake of your relationship, do not be afraid to suggest meeting up again later if you are at a conference and want to suck everything you can from it, or on a shopping trip with a long to-do list. Parting ways for a couple of hours may be the best thing to give them freedom to rest and you time to get as much accomplished as possible.

3. **Just Say No.** Peaceful Remote Controls are not keen on hectic, chaotic schedules and pressure. They value peace, serenity, and a stress-free — or at least, less-stress — environment. Think back to the restaurant example. Let's say after the 30 minute wait, you are seated, order your food, and then are served the wrong side-dish – the Remote Control will probably just eat whatever is brought and not make a fuss. They do not want to cause or witness a scene. For the Remote Control, less stress is best and they would appreciate it if you would keep that in mind.

Remote Controls should also carefully consider their calendar when it comes to activity level and involvement. Where the Hammers are the multitaskers of the world, Remote Controls perform better when they take on projects and activities one at a time. Parents of Remote Control children should keep this in mind when sign-up sheets are being passed around and peer pressure is heating up. Creating a stressful, on-the-go, non-stop environment is going to be tough on a peaceful child. It is the nature of a Remote Control to want to do things the easy way. In fact, they measure most decisions based on one question: "How much work or effort will this require?"

If you are not a Remote Control, I'm not suggesting that you encourage the Remote Controls in your life to be lazy. I am suggesting that you be realistic and recognize that not everyone enjoys life at a hard, fast pace. Be open to hitting the brakes when enough is enough.

4. **Enjoy the Ride.** If Remote Controls are passionate about anything at all it is this: enjoying and taking pleasure in life. They love to spend time with family and friends, relaxing, eating, and being in good company. Their dry sense of humor and listening ear makes them easy to be around. Play time is a must. Remote Controls like all different types of recreational activities as long as the competition tips the scale more toward fun than intensity. If things get too serious, they sense stress and will probably decide it's not worth it. Almost every male Remote Control I know has at least one hobby that satisfies a desire to pull back from the demands of work life and enjoy real life, whether it be fishing, hunting, golf, gardening, motorsports, camping, or video games. It is not that other personality types don't enjoy these activities; it is the motive that is different. The Hammer competes. The Flashlight socializes. The Tape Measure meditates. The Remote Control relaxes.

5. **Who?** Because Remote Controls are so good-natured, soft-spoken, and easy to be around, they are sometimes overlooked. In the classroom, this is the young student who never causes any trouble and does what they are told, but the teacher has the hardest time remembering their name.

As children, they often slip through the cracks and are not recognized for achievements. Into adulthood, this translates into being viewed as unambitious and weak decision makers whose opinions are easily dismissed or downright ignored.

Eventually, this easy-going person will have their fill and you will see their strength on full display. Unexpectedly, the Remote Control has an iron will and a silent, but deadly stubborn streak. It may take them a long time to make decisions or get to the breaking point in a relationship, but once the decision is made, it likely will not be reversed. Remote Controls resist change. The difficult part in circumstances surrounding a relationship is that you may find yourself shocked to learn of their disgruntled disposition. They just won't tell you about it; remember, you probably would not listen anyway.

If you are Remote Control, you probably recognize a lot of truth in the above statements. You may even be quite jaded because, for years, no one has listened to you. I am sorry. While I will not defend those of us who struggle with our listening skills, I will offer a few suggestions that will help ease the frustration on both sides. First, speak up. We cannot read your mind, but heaven knows we will put words in your mouth if you don't. Second, show enthusiasm! Sometimes the reason you feel like no one is listening is because no one feels like you really care anyway. It is easy to mistake an easy-going demeanor for an apathetic one. If you want your voice to be heard, go the extra mile to show how much you care and be open to showing uncomfortable displays of excitement.

6. **Support Staff.** In a healthy relationship, the Remote Control is the best at helping get things done. They may not be the one dreaming up all the plans and projects, but they are likely the one making it happen in the most basic ways. They are great listeners who are willing to help with a hands-on approach. For example, they may not be the one outlining all the creative details of a fund-raising event and ordering the invitations, but they will be the ones setting up the tables and carrying in the food. Their calm, cool and collected spirit is so refreshing in the midst of hyper-active, demanding types.

   Also, Remote Controls have a very hospitable nature. They want people to be comfortable. You will notice they will sacrifice their need for comfort for others, sometimes to a fault. Of all the personality types, they are the most likely to put others before self.

7. **Desire for Peace.** To obtain and maintain emotional health, Remote Controls *need* a feeling of worth, respect for who they are — not what they do — rest, and peace or a lack of stress.

E. V. E. N.
Method
Remote Control

E Emotional Need	Peace and quiet, feeling of worth, lack of stress, respect
V Visual Clues	Chameleon like, Calm, Cool, Collected, Comfort Trumps All
E Environmental Need	Area of specialization, Identification with a group, Established work pattern, Stability of the situation, Consistent and familar environment.
N Natural Desire	Peace

BONUS CLUES

Method of Control	Procrastination
Questions they want answered	How As in "How do you want this done?"
Motto	"You bro, Chill out."

"E" – Emotional Needs

*Peace and Quiet * Feelings of Self-Worth * Lack of Stress * Respect*

Remote Controls have emotional needs for peaceful, quiet surroundings, a feeling of self-worth, and a lifestyle that minimizes stress and maximizes respect. They are the epitome of "work smarter, not harder," which *can be* just as productive but might be viewed as lazy or procrastinating by other personality types; however, it is how the Remote Control gets peace. This is fueled by their natural hardwiring of having things "chill." They need their worth to be validated by others in order for their self-worth to stay intact. Of all of the personality types, the Remote Control needs their love tanks filled daily to stay focused and positive. If a Remote Control withdraws from others you can be assured it can be traced back to someone not validating their worth verbally with affirmations. They often need to hear words as opposed to actions being taken to meet their emotional needs.

Peace and Quiet

All personalities have a desire to control, it is just the different methods they choose to control with that makes them different. The Remote Control feels in control and emotionally content when they have a peaceful coexistence with the people and world around them. You might ask, "Who doesn't like things or situations to be peaceful?" The thing is that this need for peace can be taken to the extreme by a less-than-vigilant Remote Control and become an excuse for checking out of life and relationships until they wake up one day and realize they have no control and then they blow up. They resent the people they handed off control to and they act out. Let me give you an example of when a Remote Control's need for peace and quiet is taken to the extreme.

When a Remote Control man marries a Hammer woman it has the potential for disaster. He marries her because she makes him feel comfortable because she is comfortable with being in charge. He doesn't really want to be in charge of the home so he just sits back and becomes an observer of life until years later when he realizes he has no control over anything. The Remote Control man has no control at work, co-workers take advantage of his good nature, and his boss (who is more than likely a Hammer) is not impressed by the attitude of the Remote Control to work smarter, not harder. At home the wife is running the house pretty smoothly until the kids reach their teen years, and trouble is on the horizon. She wants to do what comes naturally to her Hammer personality and that is to be proactive in setting boundaries with the teens. However, the Remote Control husband who has no control or peace at work and no peace at home becomes very frustrated and will start operating in his weakness. This means he will try to control his wife through passive aggressive behavior. He does this by telling her he will support her with the mutually agreed upon punishments for the teens. But in reality he has no intention of supporting the hard line because he also needs respect and self-worth, and taking the hard line has someone not liking him very well. His need for peace keeps him from following through because the teens do what they are hardwired to do at that age – pit one parent against the other to get what they want. The Hammer wife knows this and tries everything she knows to keep the house and kids in control but she suspects the Remote Control husband is not supporting her, plus he is actually allowing the kids to divide and conquer. The Remote Control will say yes when he really means no. BIG NO NO for being married to a Hammer. The strife escalates, the Hammer wife feels betrayed and out of control because the Remote Control husband's need for peace is so great that he becomes selfish, passive aggressive and puts on his concrete shoes and refuses to do anything. Remote Controls need to be very careful as to not walk on the dark side with passive aggressive behavior. Passive aggressive behavior in the mind of the Remote Control is to do whatever it takes to bring down the person they believe is in charge or the authority figure. This can be the person who is challenging their need for peace. This behavior usually backfires on the one being passive aggressive. The need for peace by itself is fine, but when it is taken to the extreme it becomes a compulsion and it makes the Remote Control a very selfish person. They have been known to not parent their children because they do not want to be the "bad guy." Their need for peace, self-worth, respect and lack of stress will never be achieved if they refuse to understand the concept of being proactive vs. reactive. If the Remote Controls would understand that setting a proactive boundary and sticking to it with the same energy they do when they become passive aggressive and have on their (what I call) concrete shoes that stop them from taking any action, it will give them the peace they so desperately need. They create a huge mess by not being proactive. This is a very common conflict between Hammers and Remote Controls. Keep in mind that all personality types have the natural desire for control – it is simply how they go about trying to get control makes them different. The need for peace and quiet is so strong for the Remote Control that they are unable to see at times the long-term ramifications of the possibility that seeking peace and quiet can be selfish on their part. This is when the Remote Control is in their struggle.

Relationship Remodeler says: "For the love of God and all things that are Holy, Remote Controls, let your Yes's be Yes and your No's be No. Say what you will do, do what you say and follow through with your boundary setting and be consistent if you want peace. The truth is that if you do not, the Hammers in your life will treat you as disloyal liars. If you give the Hammers in your life what they need, you will get what you want – PEACE, feelings of self-worth, lack of stress and respect."

Feelings of Self-Worth

This is a tricky one to explain – the need for feeling worthy. The Remote Control personality is calm, cool, and collected. They are not extreme one way or another, and they are chameleon-like, which means they can easily blend into a crowd.

Picture that you are the parents of four children and all of them are of different personality types and have different talents. Your Flashlight child is the popular one that gets invited to everything and has tons of friends. The Hammer child is the captain of the football team and has leadership skills that come naturally. Your Tape Measure child is perfect and is always voted outstanding student of the month. Now you have your sweet, easy-going, no-trouble-causing Remote Control child who is content to go to school without making his bed or cleaning up his room, ever. When he comes home from school he heads right for the refrigerator and then for the couch to watch hours of TV and you have to nag this one to do his homework. He hardly talks but when he does he usually says, "Yo mom, chill. It ain't that serious." This child is likely to grow up and fall through the cracks his entire life. It is very important that you instill in him a sense of self-worth – otherwise he may fail to develop this in his life. He will need to feel like his parents value him, not for what he does or produces, but simply because of who he is.

Lack of Stress

You can recognize a Remote Control at your table if you are out to eat with them. They are the ones who will accept that the waitress screwed up their order and they never will say a word about it because of their need for a stress free life. They really don't have a lot of great needs that they feel strongly about one way or another because of their underlying need for no stress. They usually will not give their opinion on things if giving it will cause them stress. Remote Controls will live life in the gray if it brings them a stress-free lifestyle.

Respect

Remote Controls are middle of the road people. In school, they did not get great awards for being good, nor were they bad. Because of this, Remote Controls need respect more than the other personalities. The hardest thing about giving the Remote Controls respect is that other personalities – especially the Hammers – view respect as connected to production or work. However, the Remote Controls need respect just simply because of who they are.

I show my Remote Control husband respect by giving him undivided attention and carving out time for just the two us to do something together. Our thing is going on bike rides. I make a point to let him know that I respect that time together, so I let him see how I clear my schedule for our rides. I also let him know that I have too much respect for him to sit around and watch him not stay healthy and in shape. I have been very busy over the last few years after the kids have left home building my business and this is foreign to him since I have always been a very attentive wife waiting on his needs, hand and foot. I will admit that things have been a bit strained because I am not around to give him the respect he needs by providing this full-time care. This is hard for me because I do not need someone to give me feelings of respect of self-worth, but both my son and husband need me to do this a lot. It does not come naturally for me, but I have always done it because they need it. This is an area I pray and ask God to help me with, for both my husband and son. I ask God to help me do it cheerfully because it is important to them, and it makes them feel valued and respected by me.

Relationship Remodeler says: "To all Remote Controls, understand that we all give what we need, not what you need. This should make some sense to you all. We Hammers do not need affirmations or rely on others to give us our self-worth or respect, so therefore we do not give it to you. The real reason is we know how great we are so it does not register with us that you Remote Controls don't know how great you are. We already know how great you are so why don't you know it? Hammers need to work on affirming Remote Controls more – if we are thinking something good about you, then we need to say it out loud to you."

"V" – Visual Clues Remote Control

Chameleon * Cool * Calm * Collected * Comfort Trumps All * Relaxed
(See Visual, Vocal, Verbal Clue Sheet on Page 182)

Remote Controls are often the most difficult of the personalities to identify as their traits are not as obvious as the other personalities. Each of the other personalities lives life in the extreme: Flashlight is extremely loud, outgoing and fun loving; the Hammer is extremely strong, goal-oriented and driven; the Tape Measure is neat, organized and detail-conscious; yet the Remote Control is not extremely anything. They are balanced and consistent – and as result, harder to identify. The best way to identify the Remote Control is by process of elimination. If the person does not fit into any of the other categories, they are probably a Remote Control.

Chameleon–Like

Because the Remote Control traits are not as extreme, it is easier for them to be flexible to whatever the task at hand demands. Being married to a Remote Control, I can often witness his blending in and adapting to his situation, none more obvious than when he is at work. If he has someone with whom he is managing that is very quiet themselves, my husband will act more like a Flashlight to draw them out. If someone is over the top and loud he will back off. If someone is more on the negative side with complaining he will try to be funny. He tells me he does this to maintain balance in the work environment because his need is for peace. When he is in a social setting he will blend in because he does not enjoy the spotlight – he just wants to "be," as he puts it.

The vocal quality to the Remote Control is very calm. They have a steady, slow, warm delivery. They ask more than they tell, they listen more than they talk. Remote Controls have a gentle handshake with intermittent eye contact. They exhibit patience and they will not often offer their opinion. If you combine all of the clues then you can see and hear how they got the chameleon title.

Cool, Calm, Collected

If you have a Remote Control in your life and you are a Hammer, you will notice they bring a sense of calm to the situation where you may be all "jacked up" and agitated with something. If the energy in the room is full of tension, leave it to the Remote Control to bring a cool, calm energy to the room. The Remote Control is very diplomatic and will stick to the facts in a conflict, and they stay very collected. They are very balanced individuals no real highs or no real lows.

I can think of a situation where having a Remote Control as your leader is the best situation for all involved: in the Pop Warner organization. In our community, Pop Warner was not just football – it also had a cheer program. There were dads who coached the football teams and it was moms who coached cheer. There was constant tension between the two groups as long as I could remember; male Hammers vs. Female Hammers was a recipe for disaster. This all changed when a Remote Control man was elected president. This man had a cool, calm, collected, fair and balanced leadership style; he brought peace to the organization. As the saying goes, "Blessed are the peacemakers."

Comfort Trumps All

Whatever the occasion, the peaceful Remote Control will dress for comfort. They are usually dressed on the more casual end of the acceptable spectrum when you are talking attire. There are two words that the Remote Control takes very literally – permanent press. You know you have been in a meeting in a board room with at least one person who looks like they slept in their shirt because they took the term permanent press for its word. You can always tell the Tape Measure in the room because they have the exact opposite look. Again, look for the Tape Measure and then look for the exact opposite dresser and that will be your Remote Control. If you see someone out in public in their torn up, paint-stained sweat pants from their college days, you can bet they are a Remote Control.

Visibly Relaxed

The body language is relaxed with the Remote Controls. They have an unwritten rule: Why stand when you can lean, and why lean when you can lie down? They got their name because you can usually find a Remote Control lying on their couch with a remote control in their hand channel surfing and just "chilling."

My son had the entire basement to himself in our Ohio home. He had it set up like the ultimate man cave. He had lights on the "clapper" so he did not have to get out of bed to turn any lights off. He also had extra plastic chair runners on the carpet so he could scoot himself around without getting up. He actually had a "grabber" that was a tool that was three feet long with a grip at the end so all he had to do was lie in bed and use the "grabber" to retrieve something from the refrigerator or microwave. This is the ultimate Remote Control being relaxed. He told me "Mom you work harder, I work smarter." He is actually very right about this.

As a Hammer, I find the Remote Control difficult to relate to, but it is ok because I don't have to relate to them to give them what they need. It is all good – it is the Platinum Rule.

Second "E" – Environmental Needs

*Area of Specialization * Identification with a Group * Established Work Pattern * Stability of the Situation * Consistent and Familiar Environment*

Area of Specialization

Remote Controls tend to stick to one thing and be very good at it. They would rather be very good at one area than mediocre in many areas.

Identification with a Group

The Remote Control needs to identify with a group. An example of this can be following a particular sports team, perhaps being involved in a work related organization, church or school group. While they do not have the desire to lead these groups they are content to just "be" in these groups. These groups are where the Remote Control feels most validated. They can just blend in a group and be accepted for having something in common with other members. The over view of the Remote Control and their environmental needs can be summed up in a simple concept. Remote Controls like to be set up to succeed by knowing what is expected of them ahead of time. They can be very reliable, the" steady Eddies"' of the world. They will excel when they know what is expected of them and have the support of others.

Remote Controls do not like to be singled out for praise or criticism. They just want to be part of the group. They like it when they are part of a group so they can blend in, so just let them simply do their part and do not make them responsible for others. Also, being part of a group gives them an identity they really do not have to work hard at to maintain. They just get to be accepted for being a group member, but not necessarily for being a participant.

Established Work Patterns

You will not often find the Remote Control looking for new and exciting things to do at work. They like to know what is expected of them and do not do well with surprises. The same routine day in and day out is just fine for them and they will have success doing just that. Because they can stay focused with the established work pattern, they are steady and reliable.

Stability in all Situations

Have you ever heard that slow and steady wins the race? This was written for Remote Controls. They are not risk takers. This has them being one of the personalities with the most patience. This also means they will avoid drama at all cost. They like knowing what is expected of them; they will not give too much or too little, but just the right amount of effort.

Consistent and Familiar Environments

The Remote Control thrives on a routine. They do not resent orders and directions; in fact, they appreciate them. They need someone to lead and something to follow. When the Remote Control is in a consistent and familiar environment you will always know what to expect of them. There is something to be said about predictability.

Relationship Remodeler says: "There are two kinds of pain: the pain of change and the pain of never changing."

"N" – Natural Desires Remote Control

The Remote Control's natural desire is for peace. Peace is a great feeling that we all should want to obtain. Let's first define the term peace. What if I asked you what your definition of peace is? My definition of peace in a perfect world (which I know does not exist, but am still trying to get my Tape Measure friends to acknowledge this) is where I am in control. While we all speak the language of peace we all have different dialects. For the Remote Control peace for them is essential for their well-being. They need to be very careful because when their natural desire for all things peaceful is carried to the extreme they become very selfish individuals. It is harder to pinpoint this source of conflict because by their nature Remote Controls are quiet and people do not typically associate selfishness with the peaceful, kind, quiet nature of them. However, they will go to the extremes to maintain their peace which can result in very selfish behavior. One man's peace can be another man's strife. Do not underestimate a Remote Control when their natural desire for peace is not being met.

Bonus Clues

Method of Control – Procrastination

The natural desire to avoid conflict and keep peace is very strong for the Remote Control. When their emotional needs of respect, feelings of worth, understanding and emotional support are not being met, they will dig in their heels and silently show their strong hidden will of iron through their chosen method of control – procrastination. Carried to the extreme, this procrastination will result in passive aggressiveness. They will exhibit this control when life is filled with conflict; they have to face personal confrontation, no one wants to help, or when the buck stops with them. Remote Controls are afraid of having to deal with major personal problems, being left holding the bag, making major changes. They also dislike people who are too pushy, too loud, or expect too much from them. If you want to help a Remote Control, appreciate the stability and calm they bring to any situation. Understand they will work harder and smarter in a quiet space. Look past their slower pace and let them know what you appreciate about them. Uphold clear deadlines but do not nag or threaten. Let them know they are necessary to the team even if they produce the least. To keep them from getting depressed because they feel that no one values them or if they get overwhelmed, you can appreciate the intangibles they bring to the situation, not just what they produce. When they do try to control by procrastination, let them know you are aware of what they are trying to do and it will not be tolerated. State the consequences up front of what will happen when they try to push the responsibility or work onto others.

Questions The Remote Control Wants Answered – "How"

The Remote Control thinks in terms of *"How?"* How do you want this job done? How do you want it to look? How will I know I have done it right? They are motivated by their environmental need for appreciation (How can I gain your approval?) and service (How am I doing?). They want to feel that they have pleased you. Nothing makes them feel better than knowing they did as you expected and everything went according to schedule and plan. If you are pleased with the way things turned out, they are more pleased. Remember the thought pattern of "how" and the environmental need of "appreciation" and "desire to please," and you will be speaking their language.

I had a client tell me this story, and it serves as a good example of hearing the same conversation but focusing on and processing different perspectives based on the questions they needed answered. We will call them Sally and Bob.

Sally and Bob were out for dinner and they were on the drive home when their daughter Suzy called Bob from their home. She said, "Dad do we have a power washer?" Bob replied, "No, but check with your uncle Ed. I think he might have one." After Bob hung up, Sally asked, what did Suzy want? Bob said "She just wanted to know if we had a power washer, but I told her we did not." Sally said with anxiety in her voice "Why on earth would a twelve year old need a power washer at 9pm on a Tuesday night?" Bob responded with, "I don't know, I didn't think to ask her. It did not matter because we didn't have one." Sally took the phone and called Suzy back, and found out that it was not exactly Suzy who needed the power washer but the neighbor across the street who had spilled paint on his deck and wanted to get it off quickly. The point of this story is used to illustrate how differently the personality types see or think things through. Bob said his interest in the request was to find out *who* had a power washer.

Sally's interest was *why* Suzy would need a power washer and *how* he could help. The issue is not which of them is "right." Rather, it demonstrates that we see things through different "filters." In many instances, we can help and complement each other. This knowledge and understanding can come in quite handy when raising teens who will naturally try to divide and conquer their parents. If both parents sit down and make a pact to ask all the questions – who, what, how and why, then it makes it much more difficult to bamboozle their parents.

Relationship Remodeler says: "Changing the filter in your HVAC unit is not only necessary, it is mandatory for effective use to keep it running smoothly. The same principle applies for changing the 'filters' through which you view life and situations; it is crucial for you sustaining your relationships and keeping them running smoothly. One man's *who* might be another man's *why*, or one man's *how* is another man's *what*."

Remote Control Struggles
(See Strengths and Struggles Chart on Page 43)

Emotions: Indecisive and Have a Quiet Will of Iron

Remote Controls do not feel the need to make decisions and are usually content to allow others to tell them what to do. However, when they do make a decision, you can be sure that it is well thought out and they are not likely to change their mind. Sometimes, this stubborn will of iron can lead others to believe they are a Hammer. The truth is that the Remote Controls are the ones with the strong will of iron. They can go unnoticed with their iron will because they are quiet where the Hammer is more vocal. I refer to this stubbornness as "wearing concrete shoes."

The Remote Control is uncomfortable making a decision but when they do, it can be for keeps. It is most often seen when a Remote Control woman is married to a womanizing man. It starts out with the wife putting up with it for years. She will endure shame and embarrassment from the behavior of her husband's actions. But once she makes up her mind to leave, she will leave and not look back – no amount of pleading will get her to return once her mind is made up.

Work: Not Goal-Oriented

Remote Controls can display a lack of enthusiasm so don't expect them to be the major motivator. They do better as support persons. Their fear of conflict or pressure has them avoiding responsibility. Remote Controls have a tendency to become indecisive and overwhelmed, so they are not motivated to set goals. They resent being pushed, so don't even try.

John and Patty had a business that they ran out of their home. They were both Remote Controls, so as you can imagine, keeping or setting a schedule was a struggle for them. This can be a huge problem for running a home-based business. Staying motivated and focused to work was too much for both of them. Patty tells the story of the day they both had the courage to admit that they were not motivated to run their home-based business any longer. This was really not practical since it was their only source of income and it was a good money maker. Patty said the next day after their discussion she was invited by a friend of hers to attend one of my classes. After learning more about her and her husband's personalities, she realized they were living in their struggles and she felt discouraged until she heard me say that Remote Controls will work smarter not harder. Finally she heard something she could work with. She went home and reported to John her discovery, and the two of them put both of their heads together and came up with a plan that would serve them rather well. They remembered that when they first started their home-based business they were encouraged by a business coach to write a "how to manual" for operating their business. The coach told them that they had to plan for an exit strategy because their business would only be as good as it could be if they were running it. He was saying the business will not be worth anything if they sold it and nobody knew what they were doing or how they worked it. They pulled out the manual and updated it and put together a proposal to apply for a couple of interns at their local college. They figured if they were not motivated or goal-oriented, they could find a young Hammer or Tape Measure who is motivated by tasks and have them do all the work for the opportunity to learn how to run their own business. They did not set any goals to grow with the extra help but to take it easy and kick back while they had free, eager help with their interns. Patty sent me a letter thanking me for "showing her the way." As a Hammer I do not know how I feel about this exactly. On one hand I am not thrilled to see someone not work hard because I am motivated by how much I can accomplish in a single day. However, on the other hand I am quite impressed with their ability to think outside the box for problem solving and they took the whole working smarter not harder statement to an en entirely new level. This is a tough example of how Remote Controls are not motivated by goals at work. I guess we should really define "goals" because they certainly set a goal to work less and they accomplished it. I am confused on this one but I thought it was worth mentioning.

Friends: Stays Uninvolved and Is Indifferent to Plans

My friend Stacey is a Remote Control and she shared something with me on this point that made me have a better understanding of my research on the Remote Controls staying uninvolved and indifferent to plans.

She told me that when she is surrounded by strong Hammers who are not self aware and certainly not educated on the Four Wires of You program, it is easy for her to avoid situations in which she does not feel comfortable. She admits that she can get lost in too many details or options. But she is comfortable with having the options. She is amazed that the Hammer only sees one way to get something done. She becomes agitated that it never crosses their minds that there just might be other options. If someone else in the group steps up and presents another option, the Hammer will discard the option because it is not their idea. Stacey says she becomes frustrated and cynical and will stop investing in the process, so she will not share her ideas or insights with a Hammer. She just sits quietly and checks out.

I asked her why she doesn't just say what she wants and say it with conviction and do what it takes to have her voice heard. She laughed and said, "Because it's easier to be passive aggressive."

Those of us who are not Remote Controls may view them as uninvolved or indifferent but in actuality they are just passive aggressive – who knew. I am kidding. The truth is that if their emotional needs of being validated and respected are not being met, they will not share their ideas because they are not being heard anyway.

Relationship Remodeler says: "Remote Controls, when dealing with Hammers please have an opinion and say so. Hammers will be more apt to validate your opinion if it is more factual than feelings-related. Also, if you make it seem like it was their idea, Hammers will go with your suggestions."

Remote Control Strengths

Emotions: Good Listener

When I interviewed some doctors for this book I asked them which of the personalities made the best nurses. They replied it depends on the type work that was required. They said for example you would not want a peaceful, quiet reserved nurse in the ER or in a highly pressure filled operating room where being assertive is a plus. However you definitely want a Remote Control nurse with the elderly patients.

Dr. Pearl gave me an example of a patient he had in a convalescent home. Mrs. Tucker was her name. The more assertive, task-oriented nurses would go in Mrs. Tucker's room and try to provide care for her, but Mrs. Trucker was not having any of this "treating me like an invalid" stuff. She had lived on her own for 88 years and she wasn't going to let this broken ankle keep her from taking care of herself now. The truth was, Mrs. Tucker had lots of life experiences and was experienced in taking care of herself. The nurses would dread going in to her room because she was so snappy and just plain mean. However, the Remote Control nurse named Belinda was good with her and never had a complaint with Mrs. Tucker. Belinda said "I just sit and let her talk about her life experiences. She is fascinating and I am a good listener, which is all she needs." The other personalities naturally could not display that much patience.

Work: Competent and Steady

The Remote Control is best at making sure the group is comfortable and is always trying to find the middle ground. They stay calm when there is a crisis and they do not overreact to negative situations. Because of their lack of extreme or unrealistic responses they can see situations with a balanced view. Their inoffensiveness is a result of their low key personality.

Friends: Easygoing and Relaxed

My son had a group of friends when he was younger and they would have actual contests to see who could spend the least amount of energy from midnight on Saturday night until Monday morning 8am. They would wear heart rate monitors that measure their calories burned. The one with the least amount of calories burned would win. They thought they deserved this because after all they played football and worked hard all week with school and their activities. They also had a contest of who could design the best "man cave." They also had movie marathons and then would sit around reviewing them like Siskel and Ebert. He and his friends were so easygoing, and they could have fun just sitting around being silly boys. They made me laugh with how extreme they were about reserving their peace and energy, until they got their driver's licenses and girlfriends.

Remote Control Communication Adjustments I. A.M. Technique
(See Remote Control I. A.M. Sheet on Page 176)

While the Remote Control and the Hammer are opposite personalities, they do share something in common: neither is excessively expressive. Hammers communicate in a brief, sometimes rude manner. Remote Controls are hesitant to communicate at all, especially with those they do not know well. They are very likeable people, content and lacking any real obvious flaws in most aspects of life. Yet despite their lack of faults, Remote Controls have areas in which they too can improve their communication style.

A – Adjustment

Get Enthused

One of the easiest ways a Remote Control can improve their communication style is for them to get excited about something. Because Remote Controls are naturally low keyed and tend to measure all of life in energy expenditure, they need to be expressive – especially when someone gives them a gift or makes a kind gesture.

If you are a Remote Control, learn to be effusive. Muster up all the superlatives you can think of. Why, you ask? Because if other people feel discouraged by your lack of interest, they will eventually discontinue their interaction with you. This is never more obvious than in the work place. If you are a Remote Control and your boss is a Hammer and you show no emotion one way or the other on projects or daily tasks, your Hammer boss may interpret your lack of enthusiasm as a sign of not being loyal, not

I AM REMOTE CONTROL

 Identify

E. V. E. N.
Method

- Develop enthusiasm
- Remember "phony joy is better than genuine depression"
- Open up and share an opinion
- If you don't have an opinion then get one
- Be aggressive in your communication

Adjustments

Meet in
the Middle

Dealing with a Flashlight:
• Encourage their ideas and get excited

Dealing with a Hammer:
• Speed up your talk
• Get to the bottom line quicker

Dealing with a Tape Measure:
• Offer facts
• Back it up with documentation & data

showing appreciation, or not giving him credit for good work, which are all of the emotional needs of a Hammer. So guess what? You more than likely won't last long in that job because your Hammer boss knows nothing about you – you chose to show no emotion, and your actions are what are being judged, not your intentions. You may have had the intentions of not making any trouble and keeping your peace but you were not giving the boss what he needed – loyalty, appreciation, and credit for good work – so you did not get what you wanted – peace. The result of not showing any enthusiasm for your job: you will be dismissed because you made the other person feel discouraged by your lack of interest.

Express Opinions

When I ask my husband, who is primary Remote Control, what he would like to do, where he would like to go, or what he would like to eat, his typical standard answers are, "I don't care" or "It doesn't matter," or "Whatever is the easiest." Where I need to tune down my opinionated nature, he needs to learn to express his opinions.

After attempting to communicate with the Remote Control and receiving the repeatedly "whatever" response, most people will give up asking and just do what they wanted to do. While at first this seems like a suitable solution, it is a short term fix that creates long-term problems. I know this firsthand. Let me explain.

From the very beginning of our marriage, it was decided upon mutually that my husband would be the chief bread winner and I would be the domestic engineer who stayed at home with our two children. My role was to raise our children and to support my husband's career as he climbed the corporate ladder. My husband agreed to having me be in charge of all things related to the rearing of our children and running our home. He just wanted to be free to focus on his career. This is not to imply he was not an involved father because he very much was an involved father when it came to showing support to his children by being present at all activities and events. He just did not actively participate in behind-the-scenes decision making. He was very happy with this arrangement for years; this arrangement is what allowed for his peaceful nature to go to work and only have work to worry about. This was working for eighteen moves across country with his job and a dozen or more promotions. He was very content to take orders and not make waves with regards to choices that needed to be made about raising the children. While it had been a relief to him in the early years to not to have to make "decisions" it went terribly wrong in the teen years. If any of you know, teens are very good at dividing and manipulating parents against each other in order to get what they want. Our children were no different. They pointed out to their father repeatedly how they felt about him in their minds that their father had no opinion and I was the bully pushing him around and they needed him to "stick up" for them. My husband hates controversy and will become very strong willed when attempting to keep his peace. He would not share his honest opinion with me or the children. He would tell the kids what they wanted to hear and then tell me what I wanted to hear. He never told either of us what he wanted us to hear. He did this same thing at work and as timing goes, all of this was crashing down around him at the same time. After years of what felt to him like being an invisible person he felt worthless. While he thought in the beginning of our marriage that giving me sole responsibility of the kids and not voicing an opinion was the best and easiest thing for him to do, he experienced over time that not having an opinion will result in feelings of worthlessness.

If you are a Remote Control, protect yourself and generate respect from others. Learn to voice your opinions. Maybe you don't have an opinion on every issue. Maybe you don't have an opinion on what you do, where you go or what you eat. But there are many issues that you probably really do care about, like what happens to you at work; how people view you; how much you are valued and respected by family, friends, co-workers, etc. Start by expressing your opinions about the things that may not matter that much to you so when you do express your opinion on matters of great importance to you, people are listening and you will gain the respect of others and open up the lines of communication.

Open Up

Unlike the Flashlight, who will spit out more about their life than anyone wants to know, Remote Controls need to learn to open up and share what they are thinking and feeling. This is difficult, however, since Remote Controls are proud and stubborn with their stoic tendencies. They must realize that those cool, aloof traits are what shuts down avenues of communication, making Remote Controls seem indifferent and apathetic – to the Hammer personalities, it makes the Remote Control seem as though they are not trustworthy. If you are a Remote Control, work on sharing your ideas and projecting your voice. Remember, while your intentions of not sharing or having an opinion may be good, it is your actions you are being judged and the action says something very different.

Relationship Remodeler says: "Remote Controls, have an opinion and SAY SO if you want the self-worth and self-respect that comes as your natural hardwiring. If people don't know you through your opinions and views, you cannot expect them to trust you, respect you and give you the validation you are looking for."

EMOTIONAL NEEDS

Flashlight

Attention
Affection
Approval
Acceptance

Hammer

Loyalty
Sense of Control
Credit for Good Work
Achievement

Tape Measure

Sensitivity
Support
Space
Silence

Remote Control

Peace and Quiet
Feeling of Self-Worth
Lack of Stress
Respect

VISUAL CLUES

	VISUAL Body Language	VOCAL Tone of Voice	VERBAL Words
Flashlight • Loud • Open • Cluttered	Animated facial expressions Much hand and body movement Contact oriented Spontaneous actions	Lots of inflection More pitch variation More variety in vocal quality Dramatic High volume Fast speech	Tells stories anecdotes Shares personal feelings Informal speech Expresses opinions readily Flexible time perspective Digresses from conversation
Hammer • Energy • Body language • Function over Fashion	Firm handshake Steady eye contact Gestures to emphasize points Displays impatience Fast moving	More vocal variety More forceful tone Communicates readily High volume, faster speech Challenging voice intonation	Tells more than asked Talks more than listens Lots of verbal communication Makes emphatic statements Blunt and to the point
Tape Measure • Quiet • Closed • Neat and Tidy	Few facial expressions Non-contact oriented	Little inflection Few pitch variations Less variety in vocal quality Steady, monotone delivery Low volume, slow speech	Fact and task-oriented Limited sharing of feelings More formal and proper Focused conversation
Remote Control • Chameleon like • Cool, Calm, Collected • Comfort Trumps All	Intermittent eye contact Gentle handshake Exhibits patience Slower moving	Steady, warm delivery Few pitch variations Less variety in vocal quality Steady, monotone delivery Low volume, slow speech	Asks more than tells Listens (more than talks) Reserves opinions Less verbal communication

ENVIRONMENTAL NEEDS

Flashlight

Prestige, Friendly Relationships, Opportunities to influence and inspire others, Chance to verbalize ideas

Hammer

Freedom, Authority, Varied activities, Difficult assignments, Opportunity for advancement

Tape Measure

Clearly defined tasks and explanations, Sufficient time and resources to accomplish tasks, Team participation, Limited risks, Planning and precision.

Remote Control

Clearly defined tasks and explanations, Sufficient time and resources to accomplish tasks, Team participation, Limited risks, Planning and precision.

NATURAL DESIRES

Flashlight

Fun

Hammer

Control

Tape Measure

Perfection

Remote Control

Peace

Chapter 5
Personality Blends & Masking

People may fear that using such tools as the study of the *personalities* puts them in a box, but the truth is really just the opposite. We all start with the four basic personalities, but within each of us is a unique mix of these traits, allowing for a full spectrum of individualities. Just as all colors are made from the primary colors, the variety of men, women and children with whom we interact day in and day out have personalities that are made up of a few basics: Flashlight, Hammer, Tape Measure and Remote Control. Within these basics comes a color wheel filled with different individuals and personality types.

For example, I like to say that all Hammers are not created equal. While a Hammer has the natural desire to control and the emotional needs of loyalty, credit for good work, appreciation, achievement, certain environmental needs and strengths and struggles, it is how they go about getting these needs met that makes each Hammer unique. Another thing that can make Hammers unique is where they stand in their strengths and struggles. The natural desire and emotional needs are consistent, however. The same theory applies for the other personalities. Then you factor in the secondary personality with its natural desire, emotional and environmental needs, strengths and struggles, and you have an infinite amount of possibilities for unique personalities within each box, so to speak.

Understanding Secondary Personalities

As previously mentioned, most of us have a primary personality and a smattering of traits from a secondary personality. For me, I am sixty percent Hammer and forty percent Flashlight. The role I am playing will determine which of these personalities you will see. I must admit that the older I get, my secondary personality of a Flashlight gets bigger, especially when it comes to my dress. I do believe my Hammer percentage was much bigger when I was younger. I have confirmation that I displayed my secondary personality while I was younger because I look back on my yearbooks and the common theme with the signatures I received was how funny I was and how I made everyone laugh. This observation was secondary to the other comments of how everyone knew where they stood with me. It was noted that I said what was ever on my mind; like me or not, I was going to say what I needed to say. So it is safe to say I was a primary Hammer and secondary Flashlight.

I would like to believe our secondary personality moves into its strength as we get older. I think it is what we call "mellowing with age." The struggles of my Hammer personality have become less of a challenge the older I become, and the strengths of my Flashlight have surfaced. I credit some of this change to *learning how to get what I want by giving others what they need.*

Grasping this deeper level of comprehension will help you in your personal interactions and in your own personal growth. It is important to understand these concepts and claim your secondary personality that is truly yours.

Natural Combinations

Flashlight/Hammer

Certain combinations of personalities go together more naturally than others. The Flashlight/Hammer are one of these combinations that we call natural. They share complementary traits that make them a logical blend. Both are outgoing, optimistic and energized by people. This combination makes these people natural born leaders. They are comfortable being out front and uncomfortable being behind the scenes. This combination is energized by people. People naturally want to follow them.

While having leadership abilities is a positive, it is also to be noted that this combination should be careful that they are not overpowering people around them. A person with this natural combination of traits is upbeat and energetic, combining the fun-loving, charming nature of the Flashlight and the drive of the Hammer. The Flashlight side tones down the intensity of the Hammer side.

As a Hammer/Flashlight I am often referred to as the Energizer Bunny. I keep going and going. This can be a good quality, but if I am functioning in my struggles – or simply working with those of different personalities – I must be careful that I am not over the top. People with this turbo-charged personality natural blend are often asked if they are ADHD. I have had people say to me, "You wear me out just watching you." What can I say, other than "With all of this energy it makes it hard to sit still."

I must clarify what I mean – "being energized by people" does not mean Flashlight/Hammers cannot be alone. They can be alone when the action stops, but their energy level stops as well. It is like they have two speeds – on and off.

Other than the obvious percentages on the Personality Profile Test, it is easy to determine whether a person is more of a Flashlight or more Hammer by whether he or she is more people/relationship oriented or more work/task-focused. If they are task- focused, that person would be referred to as a Hammer. If they are more people/relationship, then they would be a Flashlight.

Tape Measure/Remote Control

This is another logical combination often found in people. Both the Tape Measure and Remote Controls tend to be introverted, pessimistic (or realistic as my Tape Measure friends like to say) and energized by solitude. Each of these personalities likes to be behind the scenes. These are the ones who like to analyze what is happening in life. For this reason, they tend to be deeper than the other personalities. A person with this combination is someone who is likeable and accomplishes what needs to be done. The Remote Control tones down what is often perceived as the picky, hard to please nature of the Tape Measure, and the Tape Measure's focus on tasks keeps the Remote Control moving.

Just as the Flashlight/Hammer needs to be careful that he or she does not overwhelm people by living in his or her extremes, the Tape Measure/Remote Control must take caution as well. Because those with this personality combination fit in the low-key camp, they need to be careful that they are not so mellow that they can slide into the classic couch potato mode, never getting up and down to do anything. Living in their strengths, the Tape Measure/Remote Control can accomplish a lot without offending anyone.

Hammer/Tape Measure

I call this combination corporate America's favorite people. The common denominator for people with this combination is their work and their focus on tasks. They are very decisive, goal-oriented and organized. When people have both their primary and secondary personality in this production based side of the chart, they are the worker bees of life. It has been said if you want something done, this combination is the one to do it.

While building my business I have had to adjust my attitude toward people with this personality combination. Before learning about myself and the differences in our personalities, I would struggle with working with this combination because I did not like how they would always point out every little problem with something and would not let go of it until they got their way. I now am very happy to know that the same personality combination that used to drive me crazy are now my "go to" people. Knowing that this combination is driven by work and tasks, I am very comfortable knowing that if there is a problem with my business they are on it like white on rice, and it also allows more of my fun Flashlight to come out and not take things so seriously. Another example of how I learned to get what I want by giving others what they need.

A word of caution to the people with this supercharged task personality, remember that people are more important than paperwork and goals. It will best serve you if you understand and respect that the other personalities bring something to the process as well. Just think about how the four chambers of the heart have to be working together for the heart to beat. The same theory applies to the different personalities; others' cooperation is essential to the process of reaching goals. So if you are a Hammer/Tape Measure, please keep in mind that you do not need to control or fix everything. Be sure to allow for grace, and liberally apply it to all things that are not exactly the way you would like them to be.

A note of clarification: Because both the Hammer and the Tape Measure are organized, people often will be confused as to which of these personalities is their primary one. However, it is important to go to the motivation behind why they are organized, the *how* and *why* they organize. Hammers organize things quickly in their heads to aid in production – they believe things will work better and they can do things faster if everything is organized. I can walk into a situation and quickly analyze it, then instantly know what needs to be done or to get the problem solved. Tape Measures do it for the inner peace of knowing that everything is perfect. They will sleep better at night knowing that all of their hangers are facing the same way and the color coding of their clothes is in order. On the other hand, the Hammer wants the hangers and the clothes color coded so they can be productive and dress faster so they will have more time to get more task done not for being perfect. Another clue that you may be more of Tape Measure is the time it takes you to organize and if you put it down on paper. Hammers have it all in their heads.

To determine if the person with this combination of Hammer/ Tape Measure combination is more one personality or the other, observe whether he or she is more outgoing or more introverted. If the person enjoys being a leader and likes to be the center of attention, the dominant personality is probably a Hammer. If the person would rather be in the background, the dominant personality is probably a Tape Measure.

Remote Control/Flashlight

While the Powerful Hammer/Tape Measure combination is corporate America's favorite person, the Remote Control/ Flashlight is everyone's favorite person! People who have this personality combination have the easygoing nature of the Remote Control and the energy and excitement of the Flashlight. Because they have the "play" and "people" elements in common, they are usually witty and fun to be with, and they seldom push for their way.

People with the Remote Control/ Flashlight combination are not goal-oriented. They will probably never be CEO of a major corporation, but they do not care. In fact, they cannot comprehend why anyone would want that much stress. They are so well liked universally that others want to help them. In fact, those with this combination often get ahead in life beyond the successes of the Hammer/Tape Measure because people want to open doors for them.

I have a friend who is Remote Control/Flashlight combination. She hardly ever gets upset. Everyone seems to love her, she is very fun to be around and she gets invited to do things with people all the time. People always seem to be buying her gifts just because she is so darn nice. She has the ability to make you feel accepted and good about yourself when you are in her presence. She is very comfortable with herself and can even laugh at herself. The Flashlight part of her makes her fun, while the Remote Control side of her brings a sense of calm to everyone. My friend can calmly go through life having more fun than anyone I know. Again, you will know if a person is more Remote Control or more of a Flashlight based on whether they are more outgoing or introverted. My friend would be more Flashlight/Remote Control, as she is clearly more outgoing.

While people with this combination of traits sound wonderful, they have reason to be cautious as well. They tend to focus on people and play and can let projects go unfinished. The Flashlight in them starts the projects with great enthusiasm only to have their Remote Control step in and stop because it takes too much effort to finish the project. You can read between the lines and see how this can also get in the way of being motivated to work hard and get ahead in life. I like to say this combination is everyone's favorite unless you have to live with them or they happen to be your son-in-law. If your little princess happens to be married to this type of man who, in your view, lacks the motivation and therefore does not earn enough to take care of your daughter, he would not be your favorite person. Society is more forgiving of women with this personality combination than they are of men. It might not be right but it is true. Regardless of gender, those with the Remote Control/ Flashlight combination must be careful to work on motivation and achievement, lest they reach a mature age and realize that they have never really gotten their lives together.

The following "Natural Blends" chart (**Page 193**) depicts some of the characteristics of the natural personality blends that we have discussed. Notice that with each personality combination, the personality combination opposite on the chart will have completely opposite admonitions. For example, Flashlight/ Hammer personality combinations need to tone down and slow down (lest they become overbearing), while Tape Measure/ Remote Controls need to be careful not to be too sluggish. Similarly, Hammer/Tape Measures need to be careful that they do not run people over in favor of a project, while Remote Control/Flashlights need to work on working.

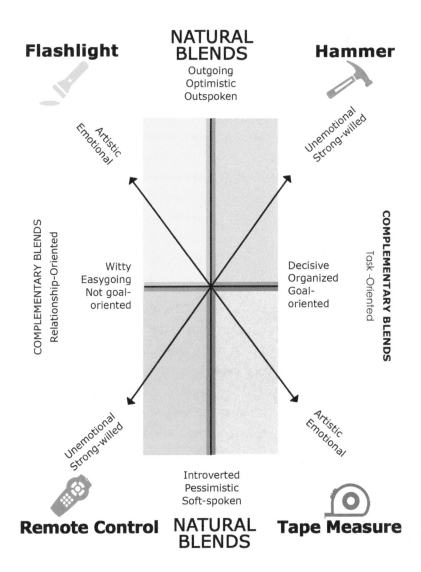

Flashlight

NATURAL BLENDS
Outgoing
Optimistic
Outspoken

Hammer

Artistic
Emotional

Unemotional
Strong-willed

COMPLEMENTARY BLENDS
Relationship-Oriented

COMPLEMENTARY BLENDS
Task-Oriented

Witty
Easygoing
Not goal-oriented

Decisive
Organized
Goal-oriented

Unemotional
Strong-willed

Artistic
Emotional

Introverted
Pessimistic
Soft-spoken

Remote Control **NATURAL BLENDS** **Tape Measure**

Opposing Blends

Opposing blends have things in common and people often think of themselves to be a Flashlight when they naturally are a Tape Measure because they are artistic and emotional. While this may be true, just like the Remote Control believes he is a Hammer because he is unemotional and strong-willed. This is confusing to people because they are diametrically opposed. It is impossible to naturally be the following personality combinations.

Flashlight vs. Tape Measure

Flashlights will cry easily as does the Tape Measure, however, always look to the motivation that has prompted the crying. Flashlights cry if someone has said something mean or hurtful to hurt them. The Tape Measure is a much deeper feeling personality and will cry at the injustices of life and the problems of the world. Both are emotional but for different reasons. Both are also creative. Flashlights are bursting with creative ideas and have many half-finished craft projects because they lose interest. The Tape Measure is very creative as well and may have half-finished projects because they could not get the project to be perfect. While they both may be very musically talented the Flashlight is more interested in the performance taking center stage but the Tape Measure is more on the perfection of it.

Remote Control vs. Hammer

Remote Controls at times believe they are Hammers because of the strong will that both personalities posses. Again always go to the motivation behind the need to be in control. For the Hammer the needs for control is very natural, on the other hand the need for control for the Remote Control is much different.

They will become very obstinate and demonstrate strong will of iron to protect their peace. While the Hammer is very vocal about their need for control the Remote Control will demonstrate their need for control very quietly and thru procrastination. Remote Controls are secretly afraid of things becoming out of control will do anything to keep their peace. Not all needs for control are created equally thus the confusion for some Remote Controls who believe they are Hammers.

Masking

Learned behaviors are a sign of growth and maturity. A learned behavior comes from not being content because at some point in people's lives, they realize that they have a need so they set out to meet it. They make a conscious choice to acquire a skill or behavior that would make them into a better person.

In contrast, a mask represents a behavior that people have unconsciously adopted for survival. This usually occurs in childhood, often to make their parents happy or to make their parents like them more. The problem with personality masks, however, is that they create an internal struggle. People may be aware of this internal battle, but since the mask is subconscious they do not understand the source of the struggle or what to do about it. Ultimately, this causes fatigue, creates stress, and can lead to illness.

We often see people who live their lives with personality masks and yet appear to be successful. So why is this a problem? Because it's not healthy for people to spend huge amounts of emotional energy trying to be someone whom they are not. And the older people get, the more difficult it is to keep the mask in place. Generally around the age of 40, people who have adopted these personality masks begin to get tired and develop stress related illnesses. They know something is wrong, but they discover who they are meant to be and realize that they don't need to wear a mask anymore. I have been told by such individuals they have always felt as if they had split personalities like Jekyll and Hyde.

If you determine that your primary and secondary personality is not one of the combinations above, then it is quite possible that you are masking a personality that is not your natural born personality.

I often tell my clients to check their natural born strengths and try to live in their strengths to "unmask." Sometimes it just takes someone seeing their natural born strengths in black and white print to have the seed planted on how they can have their internal struggle minimized, and their natural born strenghts maximized. The power of the written word is impactful. Let me give you an example.

At one of my retreats a woman was insistant she was a primary Tape Measure secondary Hammer. She had been operating out of her Tape Measure and partially masking a Remote Control. I knew just by the nature of my business what she was. I presented her with the E.V.E.N. for the Hammer and the strength and struggles of the Hammer worksheets and it was instant that she recgonized her true hardwiring of her personality and was very pleased to see it in black and white. That was very powerful for her to be given permission to operate in the strength of her Hammer and to drop the mask of the Remote Control.

Flashlight **(Real Personality)**
Tape Measure **(Mask)**

This is the most frequent masking situation I see. Because Flashlights want to be loved and desperately seek approval, they are more likely to take on masks than any of the other personalities. These inborn needs make Flashlights the natural codependents of life. They subconsciously say, if you will like me better this way, I will change. Typically, a Flashlight woman will masquerade as a Tape Measure. While she knows that she has both the strengths and struggles of the Flashlight, when she takes the Personality Profile or reviews the chart showing the strengths and struggles of all the personalities she discovers that she has many of the Tape Measure traits – in particular, she is "moody," "depressed" and "perfectionist." Yet these negative emotions are not coming from her true personality. Her moodiness and depression come from her feeling that she never measures up and is not good enough and the perfectionism comes from her trying to live up to that standard.

Some examples that may cause one to mask:

- **Parenting Mistakes**
- **Sexual and Emotional Abuse**
- **Adapting to a Spouse**

Tape Measure **(Real Personality)**
Flashlight **(Mask)**

People who are really Tape Measures but who think they are Flashlights put on the mask of a clown because they think being funny will bring them popularity, or they do it to mask the pain of a bad situation at home. On the Personality Profile, these people usually check both the strengths and the struggles of a Tape Measure, but seem to have only the strengths of the Flashlight, like being sociable, funny and popular. These people haven't acquired the Flashlight traits of being undisciplined, haphazard or messy.

Some examples that may cause one to mask:
- **Seeking Popularity**
- **Hiding Pain**

     Hammer **(Real Personality)**
Remote Control **(Mask)**

Because of the inherent strength of a Hammer, they are less likely to put on a mask. They are not as pliable as the other personalities. However, if they do put on a mask, it is usually as a result of something in their lives being out of control. Hammers have an unwritten rule: "If I can't win, I won't play the game." This mind-set causes them to subconsciously shut down if they see they cannot win, which results in their appearing to be Remote Control. I remember when I first started teaching this material and I had my good friend from high school take the test. She took the Personality Profile and declared herself to be a Remote Control – yet anyone who knew her described her as a Hammer. I remember how shocked I was to see she tested Remote Control: "Remote Control? What about you do you think is a Remote Control?" She said that she was a peacemaker, submissive and diplomatic – all qualities she possessed. But she was also controlling, could not rest, and when she walked into a room, all eyes were on her. We all in high school saw her as a Hammer, but she saw herself as a Remote Control. Upon closer look, it was easy to see when and why she had donned this mask. Both her parents were Hammers. Her father was a Tape Measure/

Hammer and her mother was a Flashlight/Hammer. Since both her parents shared the Hammer Personality, they enjoyed a good emotional arm wrestle, and my girlfriend's childhood home was filled with constant bickering. She became the peacemaker. Later, she worked for her parents in the family business. They, in turn, decided whom she would marry, and later they used their purse strings to exercise control on her life choices. My friend's parents were such a formidable force that my friend had no choice but to play Remote Control, even though she had no clue about these concepts at that time. When my girlfriend looked at herself, she truly saw a Remote Control. Yet I've never met a more imposing presence. She had played her life out as a Remote Control/Hammer, but when you looked deeper, you could see that the Remote Control was just a mask she had put on to survive in her family.

Some examples that may cause one to mask:

- "If I can't win I won't play"

 Remote Control (Real Personality)
Hammer (Mask)

A Remote Control wearing a Hammer mask is more likely to be a male than a female, although it could be either. Such a masking usually occurs when a Hammer father attempts to make his quiet, passive son "more manly." Though the father often means to be encouraging, in reality he is conveying to the child that the son is not acceptable as he is. And so, the son tries to be what dad wants him to be. Another instance of such masking can take place when a Remote Control has to take on a role of being the "man of the house" because his father is no longer there. This was the case with one man who attended my class who had qualities of both the Remote Control and the Hammer. His parents had divorced when he was six years old, and with his father gone, his mother told him that he now had to be the man of the house. Basically, she expected him to be a Hammer, and she applauded him for taking care of her. A few years later, a new man of the house moved in, and the boy was relieved of his Hammer role. The new man captured the mother's attention, and the son felt lonely and rejected. However, after a few more years, the new man left, and his mother again moved her son back into the man-of-the-house role. This occurred several times in the boy's life until he grew up and was able to move out of the house. It is no wonder that as an adult, this man saw himself as having the traits of a Remote Control/Hammer. Once he recognized who he really was, it was as if a huge burden had been lifted from his shoulders. He was free to be himself – even though he had not even been aware that he had been trying to be someone he was not.

Some examples that may cause one to mask:

- **More manly the "Head of house syndrome"**

Chapter 6
Oh the Possibilities...

I have sat for months after writing this book, creating information products and wondering if I have told you all that I could to help you improve or expand upon your relationships. Well, after many months of praying and thinking and observing more hurting people, I had my break through. No, I have not fully disclosed everything I have come to learn about people and relationships over the past seven years of hard study and soul searching and reflecting. I have left out one key relationship that is essential for your relationship remodel to be completed with a strong, secure foundation.

It's your own personal relationship with God that matters the most. While learning about the different personalities and the languages they speak is very important and worthwhile knowledge, it is your relationship with God that matters the most. I found that my daily communication with Him keeps me focused to practice my E.V.E.N. method for identification of the different personalities and more importantly, the communication part I. A.M. While reading my book, did any of you notice that when combined, the names of the program that I developed with God's grace, and love and support, ended up being I AM EVEN? I believe this was no accident, because at the end of the day Jesus was all four of these personality types in their strengths. As I did not set out intentionally to use these acronyms to make my program a lesson on God, it was led this way by the Holy Spirit. I was in a bad place in 2007 and I hit my knees and asked God to show me *Why I act the way I do and why others act the way they do.* He did just that – He lead me to study everything I could on the differences in personalities and I produced the I AM EVEN method and technique for solving relationship problems. This revelation just came to me this morning while reading my Bible as I do almost every morning. I am a personality type that needs loyalty, so therefore I give loyalty and I could not let my book go to press without adding this last chapter as my gift to you all.

With God all things are possible. Yes, with His love and grace, restoring any and all relationships is possible, even if the relationship is with you, your spouse, sibling, child, in-law, co-worker, community leader etc. Strong faith can be a stabilizing force in the midst of chaotic, difficult relationships, but faith that is out of balance or in the wrong place can exacerbate the chaos. This is exactly what was happening to me until 2007.

By developing my faith, I learned that I was here for a purpose, and that my mistakes were not fatal, and my difficulties as well as my successes provided me with the learning opportunities that helped me make the necessary choices for self-control when dealing with difficult people in my life. In summary, I had free will to make the choices I had and I needed to stop blaming others and my circumstances.

Healthy faith encourages self-respect as it stabilizes priorities on a solid foundation. I have found that with my faith, my choices are rooted in a long-term vision which allows me to be flexible so I can withstand the short-term storms. Healthy faith will help you find solutions and peace, even as you cope with difficult people. If faith is skewed and out of balance, people may become embroiled in unhealthy interactions that tear them apart. Faith done wrong makes your relationships sick and unhealthy.

I have found when most of us struggle with relationships, we have a lot of *"whys."* They bombard us constantly: Why do I stay?

Why am I treated so badly? Why do I put up with this? Why do people act the way they do? In my experience, just the faith of a mustard seed can move mountains and help you with your Whys.

I knew something was missing from my book but I couldn't put my finger on it until now. I have given you the practical advice and knowledge on *why people act the way they do,* but I really didn't give you the final key to making all of this knowledge and understanding work for you, until now. Again, I say praise Jesus that He loves me enough to continue to show me the way and the light and the truth.

Maybe He purposely lead me to put this chapter about faith at the end of my book because He wanted to emphasize that each of us has a responsibility for choices that bring healing to our damaged relationships, and what we believe effects those choices. My educated guess is that too many people try "religion" and find that their faith does not shield them from problems so they give up. They figure that their faith doesn't change the difficult people in their life. Some who are burdened with sorrow and grief will immerse themselves fully in religion and can drive others away completely with their "Bible Thumping." Yet if we reject faith because some people are out of balance with it, we are neglecting the very element for peace and reconciliation with difficult relationships.

What Faith Did for Me

Once I recognized the value of having faith, it encouraged me to seek real answers to my relationship problems. I was able to seek real answers to the *why* questions, rather than allowing chaotic emotions to control my thoughts. What I did discover was God does not resolve all of my problems, but He does offer to be with me as I work through them.

My faith has taught me:

- My life has a purpose, and based on my understanding of my personality type I am able to move forward with this purpose.

- I am not alone in this and I do not have to be the only one carrying this load.

- The circumstances in my life are not a mistake (nor are the people).

- My mistakes are not fatal. Look for the message in my mess, and also look for the treasure in my trial.

- Having a healthy faith opens my eyes to the gifts and opportunities.

- Faith changes my perspective.

- Faith helps me meet the challenges.

- Relationship struggles are an opportunity for growth.

While I am not educated in religious studies nor do I claim to be a Bible scholar, I am educated in life and in relationships. I must tell you that duct tape fixes many things but it can't fix the cracks in our foundations. Take a look at your foundation first, work on your cracks and find a way to increase your faith by developing or improving your own personal relationship with God, then use the tips and tools I provide in the practical book to repair your other relationships.

Congratulations!

On taking your first steps to becoming I. A.M. - E.V.E.N.

The goal of The Four Wires of You Program is to become a little bit of all four of the personalities in the strengths in order to become a more balanced, even person. This is hard to do until you understand – First: *Why do I act the way I do?* Second: *Why do to others act the way they do?* And lastly: *What can I do about these differences?* Doing this *will* produce effective communication with the added bonus of more fun, controlled (not out of control), respectful, peaceful relationships.

I have high hopes that you found a bit of the fog clearing with respect to being one step closer to understanding how much the emotional needs play a role in understanding yourself a bit better, but more importantly understanding others a bit better. The explanations and personal stories I shared were to help you figure out your own core needs and the core needs of others and how important it is to effective communication and learning the personality language of others.

To help you remember the E's, and any of the E.V.E.N. clues on a regular basis you can copy the chart on emotional needs and post it on your refrigerator, your bathroom mirror, or next to the computer to remind you to take a minute to think of the emotional needs when you find yourself in a potential situation for strife. Use Post-Its for the individual people in your life. Make a note or reminder in your smart phone and in your paper calendar. Ask yourself which emotional you need to give this person to reduce the static and write it down. Practicing the Platinum Rule by giving others what they need is the most powerful tool you have in your tool box for repairing or strengthening relationships.

You now have some the tools to make Romans 12:18 happen: "If possible, as far as it depends on you, be at peace with everyone."

Be in peace and with much gratitude and success,
your humble servant,

Susan Heinemann
Relationship Remodeler

Notes

Bible verses The Everyday Life Bible Amplified Version Joyce Meyer Faith Works Hachette Book Group 237 Park Ave NY, NY 10017

Wired That Way Marita Littauer, with insights from Florence Littauer Regal Books From Gospel Light Ventura, California 93006

Positive Personality Profiles D-I-S-C Personality Insights to understand yourself... and others. published by Personality Insights, Inc. PO Box 28592 Atlanta, Ga. 30358

Living Successfully With Screwed Up people Elizabeth B. Brown Published by Revell PO Box 6287, Grand Rapids, MI 49516

List of Charts and Diagrams